AUTISM DIAGNOSIS

WHAT NOW?

Another Perspective on
Parenting a Child along the
Autism Spectrum

AUTISM DIAGNOSIS
WHAT NOW?

Another Perspective on Parenting a Child along the Autism Spectrum

Winnifred Matilda Walcott

October 2014

Copyright ©2014 by: Winnifred Matilda Walcott, H.C. AADP Certified
Published by Create Space
Editing by Sharon A. Takiguchi, MS, DrPH /Jackie O'Toole
Cover Design: Jim Bisakowski - bookdesign.ca
Author photo: Sears Portrait

All rights reserved. This book may not be reproduced in whole or in part without the written permission from the publisher, except by a reviewer who may quote brief passages in a review; nor may any part of this book be reproduced, stored in a retrieval system, or transmitted in any form or by any means, electronic, mechanical, photocopying, recording, or other, without written permission from the author or the publisher.

The information contained in this book is intended to be educational and not for diagnosis, prescription, or treatment of any health disorder whatsoever.

This information should not replace consultation with a competent healthcare professional. The content of the book is intended to be used as an adjunct to a rational and responsible healthcare program, pre-scribe by a healthcare practitioner.

The author and publisher are in no way liable for any misuse of the material.

To contact the author, visit www.healthcoachwinnie.com

ISBN 978-0-9939376-0-6

CONTENTS

	Acknowledgements 9	
	Introduction 13	
Chapter 1	Hearing Your Child's Diagnosis of Autism. 15	
Chapter 2	Understanding Autism and How It Applies To Your Child 18	
Chapter 3	The Professional Team 37	
Chapter 4	Advocating For Your Child By Wearing Distinctively Diverse Hats 42	
Chapter 5	Handling Meltdowns 44	
Chapter 6	Calming Your Child 48	
Chapter 7	Feeding Your Child 51	
Chapter 8	Keep Your Child Active 61	
Chapter 9	Communicating With Your ASD Children 62	
Chapter 10	Celebrating Your Children's Birthdays 71	
Chapter 11	Taking Your Child to Different Professionals 73	
Chapter 12	Toilet Training: 76	
Chapter 13	Teaching Your Autistic Teenagers about Self-Care? 78	
Chapter 14	Spiritual Practices. 82	
Chapter 15	Self-injuries 83	
Chapter 16	The Teenage Years 86	
Chapter 17	Alternative Methods for Helping ASD Kids 87	
Chapter 18	Education 96	
Chapter 19	Services For Autistic Children. 103	

Chapter 20	Summer Camps.	104
Chapter 21	Finding the Right Caregivers	106
Chapter 22	Housing	108
Chapter 23	How the Diagnosis Affect Other Family Members	114
Chapter 24	Rewards	120
Chapter 25	Tips for Caring for the Parents	123
Chapter 26	What Happens To My Child When I Am No Longer Around?	142
	Conclusion	144
	About the Author	147
	Index	149

Poem for Parents of Special Needs Children

Hey parents of special needs children, I feel your pain.

I see your teardrops falling like rain.

As you toil tirelessly day in day out, looking for a way to make your child whole:

Have you ever thought that maybe your child is already whole and is just a gift sent to change you, to make you whole instead?

Today I bring you a message, a message of hope, peace and love.

Open your eyes and see how special you are.

You have a gift that is to be envied and not to be taken lightly.

It is a gift to show you the way.

Your child is that gift from above sent to help you to find your path, your purpose, and, to prepare you for your journey, the journey of life.

Open up to receive your gift and see the challenges as a way to prepare you to receive your rewards.

Do not frown, you are highly favored, and at the end you will receive your crown.

So cheer up parents as you care for your special needs children. Look for the lessons of life, you have been chosen for this task. Do not try to put your child in a box, these children are unique and should be free to live the way God intended for them to live.

Winnifred Matilda Walcott
Copyright © 2014

Acknowledgements

I would like to mention some very special people who helped me to become the person I am today. These special people I called my alchemists based on a book I read some time ago called "The Alchemist" authored by Paul Coelho.

The first alchemist to thank is my wonderful husband Dee; who came into my life at a very critical time when I needed love and support. Thanks darling for loving me, and for all your support.

Alchemist # two, Evelyn Drummond; thank you for assisting me with my young children and standing beside me as an emotional rock to hold on to when I needed it most. Ms. Drummond, wherever you are today, blessings to you, my second mother, I love you very much.

Alchemist # three, my youngest son, Hendy; you genuinely taught me to be humble, you taught me to be meek, you taught me to have patience, to be grateful and not to take anything for granted. You showed me how to truly let go of everything and let the universe take control, you imparted in me the ability to laugh, how to dream big and to exhibit compassion and humility. Thanks sweet child for being my spiritual guide.

Alchemist # four, my daughter Kimmie; thank you for communicating to me, the need to let go of emotional attachment, I love you, dearest.

Alchemist # five, my eldest son Anthony; you coached me to love everyone despite the fact that love could not always be returned.

Alchemist # six, Joshua Rosenthal; thank you for taking that first step, twenty years ago, and for compelling people all over the world to realize a redirected journey in life. You represent a true visionary.

Alchemist # seven, the stranger in the airplane, Nancy Nelson; thanks Nancy for conveying to me the implication of the significance of health.

Alchemist # eight, Dr. Mark Handley Derry; Expressing gratitude to you for the work you do for children diagnosed with ASD/PDD. Thank you for the numerous painstaking hours that you spent attending meetings and advocating for families. You are truly amazing, and remain very dear to my family.

Alchemist # nine: Jacki O'Toole; Jacki, before I even knew your capabilities, I knew in my heart that you would be an alchemists sent to aid me on my journey. I am in debt to you for the work you do and for the counselling that you provided me with over the past six years on this journey of life. You represent a sincerely amazing person.

Alchemist # ten; all the special needs parents I encountered while tending to the care of my own child. Each one of you touched my heart in a very special way and left marks. A special mention of Beverley, because she genuinely stands out in the care given to her child. Thanks Beverley for the outstanding success achieved with your son, he developed into a remarkable young man. Despite the fact that he will continuously need your support, I am sure that you are up to the task.

Alchemist # eleven; Max International and its' founders Mr. Steven K. Scott and Mrs. Shannon Scott; Mr. Scott, I remember five years ago at our first meeting in Utah, my family told you our story. You hugged both my husband and I, and along with many other Max Associates from all over the world, you pra*yed for us.* That special moment remains as a unique event in our lives. Thank you so very much for the ventures you perform and the vision you project to help families recover their health and financial stability.

Many other alchemists exist that I would like to mention but the list continues to be endless. Therefore, whoever touched my life in anyway; I send gratitude your way *and* an immense thank you to all.

Introduction

Twenty one years ago, our family received a blessing of the most beautiful child you ever saw. I remember cuddling him in my arms, admiring his perfectly formed feet and continuously giving thanks to the lord for him.

We envisioned great plans for our baby boy. Our dreams included careers such as a lawyer, a doctor maybe, a scientist or even a truck driver; the sky represented the limit on our goals and dreams projected for him. (These represented our goals and dreams not necessarily our child's wishes). However, when he reached the age of six, our dreams crumbled as the healthcare providers gave him a label of GDD (Global Developmental Delay), followed by ADHD (Attention Deficit Disorder), and finally ASD/PDD (Autism Spectrum Disorder and Pervasive Developmental Delay).

At that time, we lacked comprehension about what these acronyms meant and what the situation really entailed. Where do we start? What do we do? What does this diagnosis means for our son and our family? My family reacted with alarm and confusion. "What Now?"

Being a mother put me into a state of denial and blaming myself; wondering what I could have done differently and divulging that I had failed my child. I felt like a terrible mother. I experienced shame and dared not speak to anyone about our son's diagnosis and our feelings about the situation.

A dearth of information and services existed for autism at the time. Teachers possessed fewer resources to teach a child that would not sit still; or one that failed to communicate his needs effectively; or, a child that one teacher depicted as "not normal."

During my denial state, I undertook a mission to discover a cure for our son by pursuing every therapy within the perception of my senses, and, trying it. Before long our family home almost slipped through our hands because we spent vast amounts of money on a variety of therapies while searching for a cure for our son.

During trips to the grocery stores, my mind was totally focused on the needs of my special needs child and totally forgot about the necessities of the other family members.

Bedtime became the wee hours of the morning after spending evening hours meeting with various advocates and writing letters to different school board officials to get my child the proper education and services that he required to function at his best.

Our son required different activities six days per week to dissipate his high amount of energy. My husband and I took him to these activities. Can you believe that both my husband and I worked full time jobs? At one point in time, my spouse gave up his management position just to be able to cope with the myriad of appointments for our son.

This craziness transpired for fourteen years, with an occasional breather, until the placement of our son in a group home ensued. Our family reached a point of burnout. I developed high blood pressure; memory lapses, breathing difficulties and insomnia, just to name a few of my health problems. No time existed to focus on me. My responsibilities for our son came first and I resolved to help him. After my son left home, I came to the realization that I was ill. I needed help or else my own demise would come to pass and I would not be around to continue caring for my ASD child.

CHAPTER 1

Hearing Your Child's Diagnosis of Autism

So, your healthcare provider just gave your child a diagnosis of Autism Spectrum Disorder (ASD). What now? Do you drown in a sea of self-pity? Do you start asking God, or the Universe, the one question that people ask when things aren't going right? Why me God? Why my child? Do you start blaming yourself and become ashamed thinking that you epitomize a terrible parent? Or do you start considering yourself to be blessed to be entrusted with such a great responsibility? You see, a supreme being knows that you have the ability to adapt and to deal with the situation. That higher power is God, the Universe, Buddha, Allah, or, whatever you call your divine overseer. He or she knows us better than we know ourselves.

Receiving the diagnosis at first can be stressful for you and your family. The majorities of parents (especially mothers) go into a state of denial and blame themselves for being a defective parent. Parents tend to play doctor attempting everything to benefit their children, just like I did. In the process, they end up squandering lots of money on therapies; some parents even end up losing their family homes. Some fathers turn inward, keeping everything internal and fail to talk about the situation.

Failure to express emotions can be detrimental as it leads to problems in the future.

If you keep in rhythm with nature, by paying attention to all the different signs that you encounter along life's journey in this universe, you will understand how really blessed and special you are, to be entrusted with such a great responsibility. It represents a genuine gift that your higher power handed you a child with special needs, even with the many challenges ahead for you to face.

Upon interviewing a number of parents about the challenges that they have faced while parenting their ASD children, plus all the upheavals that they experience, I guarantee you that the majority of them will reveal one thing in common. This one thing happens to be their inability and lack of desire to trade their experiences for any other.

Upon receiving the diagnosis of autism for your children, the parents need to first breathe and forgive themselves. I am here to proclaim that it is not your fault. Do not for once think that you failed as a remarkable parent or, that you did something wrong. As a matter of fact you exist as an ideal parent impeccably created by God for this purpose. Do you think that God bestowed a child with special needs upon someone unfit for the job? He took great care in selecting you, deciding on the family to care for this special child. Think about it, could our higher power give this child to someone imbued with no patience, no love, and no ability to adapt and to learn? Never, for that would imply cruelty to the child. He picked you knowing that you come very qualified and possesses the skills and what it takes, regardless of what you initially thinks or feels. So cheer up; full speed ahead, and, get to work. You happen to be the highly favored, the one for this job, and a very capable parent to care for this child.

Don't ever for once feel guilty enough to shut yourself away and feel ashamed to talk about your child's diagnosis with other people. For several years, I did not want to talk to anyone about my son's diagnosis until one day at work; I overheard another colleague talking about his son being diagnosed with Autism and expressing sadness and distress about not knowing what to do next. That conversation became the turning point for me. I immediately joined that dialogue. Ever since, I take the opportunity to discuss my experience with autism every chance I get. On introspection, I found that in order for me to be authentic and to help others, I needed to share my family's story. I realized that God gave me this experience to help others living through similar life events as myself. I voice my gratitude for the opportunity to disclose my story to others.

Once you recover from the shock of the diagnosis, you need to put your emotions aside, start doing research and learn about the subject of autism.

CHAPTER 2

Understanding Autism and How It Applies To Your Child

According to Autism Canada, Autism Spectrum Disorder (ASD) refers to a complex neurobiological condition that possibly affects the normal function of the gastrointestinal, immune, hepatic, endocrine and nervous systems. It impacts normal brain development leaving most individuals with communication problems, difficulty with typical social interactions and a tendency to repeat specific patterns of behavior. The brain alterations also produce a noticeably restricted repertoire of activity and interests. Individuals residing on the autism spectrum present with varying degrees and combinations of symptoms. With the variety of possible health and behavior problems, treatment needs to be specific to that individual.

Individuals diagnosed with autism, range from the high end of the spectrum to the very low end. Some individuals at the high end of functioning need very little support, while others at the opposite end of the spectrum require a great deal of support. Being on the high end of the spectrum does not guarantee a reduction in problems. High functioning individual can become very frustrated with their lack of abilities to do things that their peers are doing. Frustration sets in and aggressive behaviors can result in them needing more support to deal with the unacceptable behaviors.

Autism diagnosis continues to rise every year. In 1970, the growth rate of autism equaled 1 in 2,500 children. In 2003, when our child finally received the diagnosis of autism spectrum disorder, the growth rate equaled 1 in 250 children. Today, 1 in 88 children in the United States of America receive the diagnosis of autism.

Leo Kanner became the first scientist to clearly define autism in 1943. Prior to this date, these children fell under the labels of feeble-minded, retarded, moronic, idiotic or schizoid. According to the National Institute of Neurological Disorder (NIH) about 36,500 of every 4 million children born each year in the United States receive the diagnosis of autism. Boys are affected with the condition more so than girls.

No two autistic children exhibit the same features of the condition. The traits and behaviors vary wildly depending upon the child. Therefore, try not to pigeon hole them into one box. Most of these individuals possess very high intelligence.

One Saturday afternoon, I met a teacher who played big brother to an autistic child. He relayed a very touching story to me. I changed the names of these individuals for the sake of privacy. I named the teacher, Johnny and the boy, Billy. I met Johnny and Billy in a Pizza Parlor. I entered the Pizza Parlor and right in front of me was Billy. He spoke rapidly and incessantly about eating his pizza and then going to a movie. Billy kept on repeating himself over and over again. A person knowledgeable about autism could within seconds describe his autistic features. I started talking to Billy about going to the movie and inquired about what movie he planned to see. He told me that he intended to see Batman, and exclaimed that he loved watching Batman.

The conversation switched to Johnny, the caregiver. I found out that Johnny taught school. He explained to me that 26 years old Billy had graduated five years ago from the school where he (Johnny) teaches and that he previously had taught Billy. Johnny described keeping in touch with Billy on a regular basis and taking him out once a month for lunch and a movie. He indicated his commitment to Billy's happiness.

Johnny went on to tell me that Billy's parents were told by his doctor that he would never speak. One day, Billy just started talking and has yet to be silent. He just loves speaking. As Johnny related that story he released a big chuckle with Billy laughing as well, in a mimicking state.

Johnny further described teaching special education classes for students along the autism spectrum for the last 15 years. He has yet to find a case wherein two autistic individuals possess the same characteristics.

I found Johnny's story very touching. He displays a generous heart to perform work as a special education teacher. All the children, with the opportunity to be in Johnny's classroom, should gain multiple benefits from such a wonderful, kind, loving and compassionate human being as their teacher.

After this heartwarming story, let's look at just a few of the traits of individuals along the Autism Spectrum.

Impairment in communication

Some autistic individuals exhibit a non–verbal demeanor, while others are quite verbal with others around them. Verbal individuals with high functioning abilities still can display problems with communication. For example; they might read very well but not comprehend what they read. On the other hand, they might need time to grasp what the other person is saying to them. When these events occur, the individuals can become frustrated and express their exasperation with in-appropriate behaviors. The individuals receive punishment instead of understandings regarding their inappropriate behaviors. Autistic individuals don't understand why they are being punished, when their outburst or, altered behavior relates to an attempt at communicating their needs. Undesirable consequences can occur with these individuals turning inward and ceasing to speak altogether. This situation can be very discouraging for them and others, such as parents, caregivers, teachers, etc.

Lacking social skills

Children along the spectrum sometimes lack the ability to initiate play and tend to follow side by side, with a play mate. They lack the capacity to approach another person and ask to join in a project or play a game. This lack of skill can frustrate the parents. However, great coaching and teaching can provide an avenue for some of the autistic individuals to develop these skills; whereas, others will continue to be unable to do so due to underlying biological deficiencies. Autistic children may like isolation, playing alone and completely disregarding other children that play in nearby proximity. The autistic child acts like the other person isn't present. If another child tries to initiate play, the autistic child might or might not respond. In spite of this, the autistic child refrains from being the first person to make the contact. These autistic children do not know how to start a conversation, and the child without autism has to carry on the dialogue and urge the autistic child to participate.

Parents are caught between a rock and a hard place. Are we hurting our children when we attempt to change them, to conform to our ways and thought process? What if it switched around and the autistic child changed us to live in their world, how would we feel? What would we think or do? I believe that God, an infallible being, generates no mistakes and that our supreme being puts us here for a reason. Parents should ask for divine guidance to teach their autistic children and in turn, be open and responsive to receive the *answers*.

Limited eye contact or none at all

The autistic child tends to gaze anywhere but not into your eyes. If you converse with them, the child's eyes wander about, shying away from your direct line of vision. The gaze away from your face represents her way of comprehending the situation. When the child looks away, she uses hearing to better understand your conversation. A critical key point highlights the necessity to speak slowly when talking to them. Wait for the child to respond before you move on. Autistic children process information at a slower pace than normal children do. The process to communicate can be very lengthy with the child with autism, but it reduces the frustration for all involved.

Referring to themselves in the third person

Some high functioning verbal children communicate their desires by speaking in the third person. Using the people in the scenario presented previously, for example, the child will say Johnny wants this pencil or, Johnny wants that eraser. For food request, the child enquires about your hunger, "Mom would you like to eat now?" hoping that, you know that it refers to him.

Our son asked us, "Mom and dad, are you going to eat now?" referring to his own hungry state. Eventually, my husband and I became experts about understanding his cues. We knew immediately how to interpret his gestures to us. A problem arose with the multiple methods of communicating with him. We conversed with him one way and the teachers connected with him another way or, sometimes failed to exchange words at all. When the teachers, or other people, failed to respond to his needs by using his family's technique of conversing, he became frustrated and confused and acted out with inappropriate behavior. The school would call us to come and pick him up. We were told by his teachers that his unacceptable behaviors disrupted his class and he has to go home. Does this situation sound familiar to anyone rearing a child with autism?

Touching

Some autistic children dislike being cuddled or to be touched. If you feel like hugging or touching them, prepare them first by asking permission. You might want to say something like, "Billy I am going to give you a hug" or ask, "is it okay if I touch you Billy?" and wait for permission. If you fail to ask for their consent or discuss the situation with them, unacceptable behaviors might erupt and you might not understand why.

Sensitivity to clothing

A variety of autistic children develop inability to tolerate (sensitivity to) certain textures of material next to their skin.

Some children detest wearing rough material like denim jeans. They like specific types of fabrics such as soft cotton material. Depending on the age of the children, allowing them to choose their own clothing might help to avoid problematic behaviors that can occur when a specific child becomes exposed to a piece of clothing that makes them itch or fails to be gentle next to their skin.

Limited choice of foods

Autistic children often like eating the same food over and over again. These children enjoy certain texture in foods such as crunchy types of foods. Certain individuals even crave junk foods and fail to eat healthy foods. Others show a partiality to fruits and vegetable. More details about foods will be explained in a later chapter.

Impulsivity

Most individuals with autism display high impulsivity and execute activity without thinking. A child may sit still one minute and suddenly jumps up and head for the door to go to the bathroom. Some caregivers or the teachers suspect that the child is up to no good, and completely unaware of what that child is thinking. They immediately call the child to go back to her seat. The child realizes that she must continue to the bathroom or risk soiling her clothes. All of a sudden, commotion erupts as the teacher or the caregiver chases and catches the child. Unfortunately, the child receives blame for displaying disruptive behavior, and then the teacher disciplines the youngster. Note that the school could end up suspending the child, even though the fact was that, the behavior arose from impulsive nature of the child to take care of a basic and urgent need to use the bathroom. One cannot blame the child or the caregiver/teacher for the incident, because the child acted out the innate nature of her condition and the adults in the situation responded out of ignorance. The key resolution to this situation involves education about autism for all relevant parties.

Other impulsivity situations arise regarding the child's desire for a toy and the parent denies it. The autistic youngster becomes distressed and runs out into the middle of oncoming traffic without thinking, even though the parents taught the child about the rules of the road previously.

This situation shows the child is not thinking, but, acting impulsively, without bringing to mind the potential dangers of this event.

Now, what do you do in this situation? Of course, the first concern must be safety. Once safety is established education takes center stage.

The first type of education involves the child. Using a format of videos, the child sees images, of what could happen in such an event. Another method is using role play with the child to demonstrate to the youngster how dangerous the situation is.

The second type of education encompasses a discussion with the parent, caregiver and teacher. This education format takes the format of brain storming. Brain storming with all the involved parties produces a plan of desired and effective action to prevent such a situation from happening again, along with how to deal with the situation if it does occur in the future.

Tends to be isolated and in another world

Have you ever noticed your child gazing at some object or thing, but the item does not exist? The autistic individual often displays this behavior. When you ask them what are they looking at, they suddenly stop gazing and become more aware of their surroundings.

Regression

Sometimes, the autistic child may meet most of her two year old growth milestones on time, but then starts to regress. An example involved the case of our son. He conversed with us up until the age of two then he started to regress, reverted to making babbling sounds and pointing at things that he desired instead of using words to request these things.

Great memory

Most children with autism demonstrate high intelligence and possess great memory. The youngsters memorize a variety of things such as the weather, the time, different types of cars, history, numbers etc. Avoid apprehension or pity for your children because of their special needs. Discover what the children excel at and then work to improve their abilities in that special area of expertise. By helping them to develop their talents, this will boost their self-esteem and provide them with a platform to build their life upon. Trust me on this one; the autistic children will thank you for this in the long run.

Problems with the ears

Most of our autistic offspring develop ear problems such as infection, earache, or the like. If possible, stay away from antibiotics as much as possible, because this medication breaks down the immune system. It is better for your children if you simply work with your General Practitioners or Primary Healthcare Providers to uncover the root cause of the problem. Once you determine the reason for the ear disorder, you can then use one of the many ways of helping the children, such as working with your Practitioners, Homeopathic Healers, or Naturopathic Doctors.

Some children fear noises produced by vacuum cleaners, hair dryers and sounds during flight in an airplane, to name a few. The ears problems could simply be pressure built up in the ears, allergies or, the beginning of a common cold. Whatever the cause, your General Practitioners will get to the root of the problem. If the child lacks the ability to communicate, you may not discern what the problem is. The problem might just be that the child dislikes travelling on an airplane.

Someone once related a story to me about their family going on a vacation but, their autistic child preferred not to want to travel on the airplane even though he expressed excitement about going on vacations.

This family planned to take the trip by air transportation and that trip represented the second trip by air for the autistic child. While at the check-in counter at the airport, the youngster started to display inappropriate behaviors, behaviors so extreme in nature that the security arrived to control the situation. The family ended up cancelling the trip, because the child could not travel at that time.

The mother related to me that the situation devastated the entire family. The child being fourteen years old at the time faced some setbacks in his life. He turned inward and stopped talking due to the disappointments.

The mother disclosed to me that when the child reached nineteen years old, he began speaking again. She described her son verbalizing that, when he was older he planned to build a bridge from their hometown to all the other countries in the world, so that he would be able to travel to those countries. She chatted with him and told him that he could also travel by airplane or ship, but he told her that he preferred not to travel by airplane. She probed further and found out that, when he travels in the airplane his ears feel funny and hurt. The ear symptoms explained the reason for the child's inappropriate behaviors at the airport previously. The child explained the reason for not wanting to travel in the airplane at that time, as due to the discomfort in his ears. He used his behaviors to communicate his needs so that his parents spared him from going on the airplane. The major issue here involved his unawareness about the seriousness of the consequences for his behaviors. In the child's mind, he received punishment for no apparent reason, which includes hospitalization and medication, when he was only communicating his wishes of not wanting to go on the airplane.

This event occurred for one simple reason; the absence of clear communication. If that child could have communicate his needs about his ears problems, this fact could possibly have saved everyone frustration, including preventing the child from hospitalization and medication that actually cause more problems.

Obsession with things

Most children along the autism spectrum become very obsessed with different things, such as riding in the car; while others scream and kick not wanting to go into the car. Most parents do not know why these children react to the car ride the way they do. Some believe that the car produces a calming and soothing effect on the children, and others believe that the vibration that occurs while the car is in motion upsets these children.

A parent disclosed to me a story about her daughter. She could be having the most difficult day, but as soon as she gets into the car, she became very calm and more aware of her surroundings. The mother said that she knew exactly how the radio worked in the car and became fascinated with the volume by turning it up and down, changing the stations and having the time of her life. Some parents believe that the children feel more secure and safe in very tight spaces such as in a car.

Another parent explained her grown-up autistic daughter, revealed to her, her fear of the car and how she feels very sick when it is in motion. This lends credence to the theory that no two individuals along the autism spectrum possess the same traits.

Autistic children often are obsessed with watching a particular movie over and over, or playing video games. One parent told me about his young son becoming obsessed with the movie, *Toy Story*. The son collected all the characters, including articles of clothing of Woody and Buzz. He occupied his time by rewinding a certain section of the video over and over. That parent went on to explain that his son did not like watching television. The only shows that he watched on television were *Barney and Friends*, *The Magic School Bus* and *Arthur* and he was stuck on these shows.

Difficulty with hand writing

Some autistic children write with great difficulty; others write very large, or off the line; some develop problems holding a pen or pencil, and some only write in capital letters. If your children's hand writing drives you crazy, save your children and yourselves frustration, and get them a laptop computer. Most school districts will provide your children with a laptop computer once they reach school age. You need to advocate for it, or, if you can, buy it for your child, that's even better.

Neatness

Children with autism prefer neatness. These individuals enjoy putting things in a certain way and get off track when anyone changes the order of things for them. They even start a tantrum and you have no idea why they generated the tantrum. By paying close attention to your child, you will notice that their preference for everything is neat and tidy, or in the place they put it.

I believe that these autistic children get quite confused when a mess or clutter occurs. It brings to mind my son always organizing all the shoes nicely by the front door. As soon as someone comes in and leaves their shoes out of place, he picks them up and places them in order. Even his room always remains neat and tidy.

Echolalia

Some autistic children with the ability to speak start out by being echolalia. Echolalia means when you ask these autistic children a question, they repeat the question back to you as their answers. For example; when you ask them how was their day at school? The children will repeat "How was your day at school?" for their answers, or, they might repeat phrases from their favorite TV show characters, or in my son's case he used phases from Buzz Light Years' characters, Woody and Arthur.

As the children get older, they fail to grasp how to formulate their own sentences, or to organize their thoughts. They begin to use one or two words when responding to a question. Yes or no become their favorite words. Sometimes it becomes very hard to comprehend when no is no and yes is yes. The parents develop skills to understand their children and learn how to communicate with them, because they spend the most time interacting with them. Problems arise when other people care for the children and the communication barrier begins.

Pacing

A number of autistic children spend a considerable amount of time pacing back and forth. The pacing makes many people really nervous. I find that when this activity occurs, something renders them unhappy, or uncomfortable, or, they desire some undetermined thing. A select few even walk in circles several times per day.

The parents can gently divert their children's attention to a different task. If the parents catch the children pacing before they get to an extended level in the pacing, the youngsters can be diverted to an interest that they enjoy. This action may diffuse a temper tantrum before it materializes.

Dislike changes and transitions

Most individuals along the autism spectrum like regular routines. Therefore, when scheduled activities change for them, confusion and disorientation sets in. One can attempt to prepare them for changes and transitions as much as possible; however, at times the parents possess no control over the situation. The parents must teach them that situations occur un-expectantly and go on to explain how to act in those situations. This issue will be discussed again in a later chapter.

Competitiveness

Most highly functioning autistic children, behave very competitive and perform poorly at team sports, but excel in competitive sports such as track and field, tennis or cycling. However, it must be noted that suffering defeat, upsets them and they end up throwing temper tantrums. Telling them a social story about athletic outcomes, represent a great way to prepare them for the events. Explain to them that occasionally people win and sometimes they lose, but it is still okay.

Difficulty Sleeping

It is imperative for all children to get a good night of sleep. Sleep assists with growth and proper immune system functioning. Difficulties sleeping at night affect most children along the spectrum and this in turn affects daytime functionality. Lack of sleep intensifies the challenging behaviors of the children, which in turn adversely affect the children and the care-givers.

Did you ever notice that when your child exhibits poor sleep, the next day the behavior deviates from normal and that day the child struggles with more difficulty throughout the day? Some of the reasons for sleep problems in children along the spectrum, could be related to, but not limited to; night terrors, seizures, allergies, sleep apnea and gastro esophageal reflux.

If you suspect that your child has a sleeping disorder, what do you do?

The first thing to do is to write in a diary the sleeping pattern of your child over a two weeks period. Gather as much information as possible over these two weeks. Gather such information as; the number of waking hours, the number of sleeping hours, the endeavors prior to bedtime; note if the activity was calming for the child, or, record if the activity stimulated the child, list the TV programs watched by the child before going to bed. What foods did the child ingest that day?

Describe the coziness of the child's sleeping arrangement? This information helps you to determine the reason for your child's inability to sleep.

Once data collection of the above information is complete; make adjustments in the schedule, diet, sleeping arrangements and the activities a few hours before bedtime. If problems with sleep continue after changing the child's diet, bedtime routine and providing a cozier sleeping environment, it is time to converse with the experts. Make an appointment with your child's pediatrician to speak to him or her about your concerns. The healthcare provider will make the necessary preparation for the child to see a sleep specialist to do a series of tests.

A parent chatted with me once about her child having problems sleeping. She happened to describe the types of behaviors seen in her child and she mentioned it to her grandmother. The grandmother advised her to give the child a tea made from raw cacao just before the child's bedtime. After she started the tea routine, the child rarely woke up at night. That being said, it makes sense that we all need sleep to repair our cells, but it doesn't matter when you sleep. It could be day or night. The key for enough rest is to have seven to eight hours of uninterrupted sleep. Having the room completely dark when we sleep continues to be an essential element to raise our serotonin level, thus encouraging a healthy sleep pattern.

Repetitive Behaviors

Most autistic children perform repetitive actions by repeating a function over and over again. I am not sure as to why, but I am sure that a logical explanation exists somewhere.

This one autistic young man that I encounter on the bus each day, keep saying the same thing over and over "Have a cup of tea." Every day he repeats the same words to everyone in close proximity to him. People react to him in different ways. Some totally ignore him, some move further away from him, some tell him to shut up, some act scared of him and a very few carry on a conversation with him. Once you start chatting with him, he starts to incorporate additional words like, "What is your name?" "Can I go to work with you?" He always reverts back to the original statement "Have a cup of tea."

Another time on the train, I noticed, an autistic lady boarded who just mumbled and hit herself. Some people on the train looked scared upon seeing this lady and moved away from her; while others just stared and gave her the eyes; you know those eyes that I am talking about. "How dare her behave like that and be on the same train with us?" Just imagine being on a crowded train in close proximity to a person who does not speak and keeps on mumbling and hitting herself. She stood there a good five minutes until I asked someone to give her their seat. The minute the lady got up; the autistic lady sat politely down and all the abnormal behaviors disappeared. Seeing her sitting there, you would never know about her autistic condition. A few of the ladies on the train inquired as to how did I know what to do? I responded with "I am experienced in that field." The point being, she did not know how to ask for what she needed.

Frequently, society does not understand differences, which indeed represents a sad day in our civilization. The problem appears to be a lack of understanding and familiarity with Autism Spectrum Disorder. Instead of spending the time and energy attempting to change these individuals, why not spend some of the time and effort educating the public about autism, how it affects these individuals, and reveal how a person can become part of these autistic individuals' lives? This education could lead to respect for the autistic individual and assistance to this vulnerable population. In this scenario, the world could be a safer place for not only the autistic individuals but for everyone.

Acting age appropriate

Autistic children normally fail to act their age. Most of them function at a lower level than their age, making it especially hard for them to interact with peers of their own age. For example, the chronological age of the child might be age ten, but developmentally the child functions at age two or three. This developmental mismatch makes it extremely complicated for everyone involved. The child feels more comfortable playing with youngsters of their developmental or functional age.

Another example describes the same ten year old child from the previous paragraph. He desires an item like a toy airplane, but the parents deny it. In response to the denial, the child throws a temper tantrum like most two years old. Since the child looks like a ten year old, everyone expects the child to act as a ten year old. When the child fails to act age appropriate, the teachers, parents or caregivers forget about the functional age of the child and in most cases punish the child.

It becomes crucial to emphasize compassion and education while working with autistic children and the involved adults.

When a mismatch of the chronological and development age in children with autism occurs, adults must take into consideration that the child might be one age, but could be functioning at a total different age.

Multiple Diagnoses

Individuals with autism could possess more than one diagnosis. Dual diagnosis refers to an individual developing two health conditions. The additional diagnoses could come from a combination of different complications. A number of autistic children suffer from both ASD and ADHD. According to Keath Low of About.com, research shows that about 30 percent of young children with ASD (Autism Spectrum Disorder) also acquire Attention Deficit Hyperactive Disorder (ADHD), as well.

Dual diagnosis creates a greater risk for an increased level of impairments. One mother declared that her child developed both autism and Down syndrome and it became very difficult to decide which complication to treat first. My suggestion would be to work with your child's healthcare practitioner to address the issues that causes the most complications.

These characteristics represent just a few of the unlimited traits of individuals along the autism spectrum. Now that I have introduced you to the subject of autism, it becomes time for you to gather a team of professionals.

CHAPTER 3

The Professional Team

Your *professional team should consist of, but not be limited to the following individuals:*

Family Doctor/General Practitioner/
  Primary Care Provider
Behaviorist
Dentist
Optician
Dietician
Health Counsellor / Health Coach
Educational Psychologist
Occupational Therapist
Speech and Language Therapist
Clinical Psychologist
Pediatrician
Psychiatrist
ENT specialist
Etc.

You look at this list and exclaim to yourself that this inventory represents a lot of people. Why do I need them all? Why can't I just interact with one individual who understands my child's needs? Let's discuss why you need these professionals.

Each one specializes in different areas of your child's life. Here are each person's roles.

Family Doctor, Primary Care Provider or General Practitioner: The family doctor, primary care provider or, the general practitioner denotes the first point of contact for you and your child. These providers assess your child and make referrals as necessary to other professionals and specialists. Some families choose to use the same doctor or general practitioner that has been in the family from generation to generation. Since the same provider records the health history of each family member, keeping the same doctor for all the family members makes it easier for you and the doctor.

Behaviorist: The behaviorist team supports you by assessing the child's challenging behaviors and develops a plan of action to address the behaviors. In order to access this treatment, you need a referral from your family doctor, other health professionals or from a social worker.

Dentist: Parents need to take their children to the dentist on a regular basis as the autistic child might not be able to tell you about their ache or discomfort. In this case, the dentist will detect any problems before a big issue arises. If at all possible locate a dentist that specializes in working with autistic children. These specialist dentists normally understand the traits and problems of autistic youngsters and possess the expertise and techniques to work with your child.

Optician: The optician assesses any problems with the child's eyes. Once the eyes are tested, you will be able to rule out any visual difficulties in your child.

Dietician: A dietician provides advice on diet and nutrition for your child and the entire family. This individual describes the amount of nutrients for growth and development.

***Health Counsellor*:** A health counsellor (Health Coach) not only provides you with information regarding health and nutrition, but, holds you accountable for the health goals that you set for yourself and your family. These individuals teach you about the concept of primary foods (A trade mark of The Institute for Integrative Nutrition) which plays a big role in helping you and the family care for your ASD children. More on this topic will be discussed in a later chapter.

***Educational Psychologist*:** These professionals assess your child's educational needs especially in light of the delayed development of many autistic children. Usually they are employed by the school board. A number of the educational psychologists work independently but can be very costly. However, if you are a parent looking for a non-biased assessment for your child and you can afford the cost, it is always advisable to get it completed independently.

Occupational Therapist: These professionals help work on the day to day needs of your child. For example, some individuals suffer from problems with certain textures of clothing, problems with the environment, issues with repetitive motion, etc. These professionals assist with therapeutic techniques and make recommendations for adaptations to the environment. Our son endures sensitivity to certain textures in clothing. He refused to wear jeans and only wore clothing made from cotton or jersey material. The occupational therapist was the first to recognize the problems with fabrics and made appropriate recommendations for us to follow.

***Speech and Language Pathologist*:** These professionals examine the child's language, speech and communication ability and then prepare recommendations for the parents, care-givers and the teachers to adhere to. These professionals also work to implement alternative communication systems to benefit the child.

Contact your school principal, or family doctor for referrals for your child to see a speech and language pathologist. If required, or necessary hire one privately. Always remember to obtain recommendations even if you hire privately as you need someone with a suitable track record.

Clinical Psychologist: These professionals take responsibility for diagnosing ASD and can offer follow-up services when a child displays behavioral difficulties. Clinical psychologists write valuable behavioral plans. Access this service through your school board, agencies that deals with ASD/PDD, or, you may hire one that is in private practice.

Pediatrician: Parents need to find a high-quality pediatrician. This practitioner helps with tracking your child's development. They also contribute to the diagnostic process and work with you and your child in providing supports. When hiring a pediatrician, ask your family doctor, or, general practitioner for a referral.

Psychiatrist: These mental health practitioners also provide diagnosis of your child's condition and offer follow-up services to aid your child if necessary. These professionals differ from psychologists in that they prescribe and monitor medication for your child, in case of severe behavior and mental health issues. You need a referral to access these professionals, or, you can hire a psychiatric practitioner in private practice.

Educational Team: Remember to always plan a meeting with your child's school to discuss your child's needs. In most cases, you will be invited by the educational team to a meeting prior to your child starting school. This team possibly consists of the school principal, or, the vice principal, the special education teacher, the special needs assistant, the school psychologist, and representatives from the school board, or, even the ministry of education.

Support Group: It benefits you greatly to find a support group or, establish a parent group to meet your needs. Trust me, you will need support! The challenges vary throughout the growth of your child and other parents experience the same complicated encounters. The value of support groups lie with the sharing or solutions to grueling situations.

CHAPTER 4

Advocating For Your Child By Wearing Distinctively Diverse Hats

Now, you have your team in place, all is well, and you expect smooth sailing ahead, right? Wrong! Your actual work is just beginning at this point. You now commence wearing lots of different hats as you care for your children.

Along with your parental role, you have now become an advocate for your child. At this time you begin learning the skill of advocating. If this activity makes you uncomfortable, request a referral to a good advocate from your team or hire one privately. To discuss your options, speak to other parents that went through the process, or, search on-line for organizations that carry out this activity. Before making a decision, ask to speak to some of their past clients, if possible. Remember, 'Buyer Beware'!

Every child has the right to get a proper education. Unfortunately, an appropriate education does not materialize automatically. You need to become familiar with the educational laws in your region to discern what your child's rights to a proper education will be in your area. With knowledge about the law, you acquire the ability to advocate your public education system regarding optimal solutions and opportunities.

You become the "captain of the ship" navigating the variety of systems and services of benefits for your child. You need to attend scores of meetings for your children. The point here is for you to document everything. Take descriptive notes and keep meticulous records as you might need the information for later use. Every time you speak to someone new, you will need to repeat your story over and over again. It becomes annoying at these meetings to be asked the same questions each time you speak with someone new or you complete a form. You always have to answer two particular questions: 1. "Are you married or single?" 2. "Where was your child born?" This usually disturbs me to no end, and you will likely experience similar stressors.

You really need to attend all the meetings about your child. No meeting should be held regarding your child without your attendance. Remember you retain the right to take a representative with you to these encounters. It can be very challenging at times to work with your school team. Keep in mind that the objective of the game with your school team is the establishment of a good working relationship so that your child's needs get met. Refrain from being emotional. If parents become emotionally upset, the school labels them as problem parents and puts them on the school's blacklist. You must avoid becoming blacklisted at all cost in order to get your child's needs met. Focus your energy on helping your child and avoid wasting it by fighting with your school team.

Raising a child with autism can be very costly as your child requires the services of different therapist, doctors' appointment, after school programs, etc. The government provides certain services and benefits to help parents with these expenses; but you must research in order to find and access these services. One of the best ways involves doing a google search under 'funding for autism,' or, asks your pediatrician for referrals to these services. Each country, state, and province differs, so do your investigation.

CHAPTER 5

Handling Meltdowns

New parents might ask, "What are meltdowns?" Meltdowns refer to emotionally inappropriate behaviors (throwing a tantrum or, physically fighting with a parent, or, caregiver) that your child exhibits at home or in a public arena. These usually occur because the child wants something and is being denied the thing desired. Now the child is exhibiting communication issues, or, maybe wishing for control of a situation that they are unable get.

These meltdowns potentially last for a protracted time until the child gets his own way, or, complete exhaustion sets in. The meltdowns project a pretty ugly sight as these children expand to twice their strength or more during these episodes. The child normally acts totally out of control and cannot be reasoned with during that time.

Meltdowns in autistic children represent a challenge for the parents, especially a meltdown occurring in public places like a mall, or church. You need to remain calm during this process. You must find a way to be composed, use a calm tone of voice, but be very firm in a loving way. Refrain from chasing your child, as some children like to play the chase game. When a meltdown crops up, some children tend to like running around.

If you pursue them, they keep going and bad things potentially could happen such as running out into traffic and sustaining injury.

Maintain control of the situation and never give in. Some parents tend to give in to the child's behavior just to avoid embarrassment. Never give in. If you do, you teach the child that it is okay to use that particular behavior to get something she wants. Unfortunately, they grow up and continue to do the same thing. Later in life, the behavior becomes harder to control, because their strength increases and the behavior become ingrained over a period of time.

When my child exhibited meltdowns in public places, I learned overtime to become desensitized to the reaction of other people. Individuals looked at me with a very strange look on their faces. One lady once said to me, "Why don't you teach your child discipline at home?" My attention was diverted elsewhere at the time and I could not respond to her. I appropriately just kept on concentrating on my child. You can't blame these people as they possess no clue about autism, do not know autism, nor you or your child. The people observing the meltdowns mattered not at all; neither their thoughts nor actions affected me. My major concern aptly centered on getting my child to settle down.

When your child reverts to one of those meltdowns, if at all possible, move him to an area with less traffic, like a family washroom. Sensitivity to noise might be the reason for the meltdown.

I invite you to envision the following scenario with me. *You plan to go to the shopping mall with your child. You prepare him for the trip and he exhibits enthusiasm about going to the mall. Twenty minutes after arriving at the mall, your child starts throwing a tantrum. He pulls at his ears and screams his head off (hypothetically speaking). He runs and hits everyone in sight. You become very upset and frustrated. You wonder, what is wrong with this child. You eventually catches up with him, takes him to the car, and he settles down completely after ten minutes.*

You fail to understand why he developed a tantrum. You ponder a moment and figure out what might be the problem. It's his hearing displays sensitivity to noise! He picks up all the sounds of people from all directions coming toward him in the mall. Remember, he is unable to express his feelings to you. He just wants to run away to escape the noise, but no one could understood him, not even you in the beginning.

The next time you arrive in a crowded space and this happens, remain calm. Remove the child from the crowded area. Please do not pay any attention to whoever might be looking at you and your child, as your first priority is your child. Over the years, I learned how to keep my focus on my child during a meltdown and to forget about others watching or making nasty comments.

Once the meltdown resolves, you should record the incident for future reference. Think about everything surrounding the event. What was the antecedent that led up to the behavior? Ask your child about his feelings prior to his behavior if the child can speak. Was he in pain? Was something occurring in the environment? Did you promise the child some item and failed to follow through with your promise? One thing I know for sure about autistic children: if you promise them something, you must keep your promise to them. Remember, the child with autism does not understand that things can change. We must work to teach them to handle disappointment when it occurs.

Role playing with your child and chatting about social stories represents great ways to teach them about changes and transitions. As a matter of fact, social stories really teach children in a way that they will understand. Meltdowns at home remain much easier to handle than in a public arena, as you maintain more control over the environment at home.

Avoid spoiling your children. Be consistent with your discipline, but remember that their attention span remains very short and you should only discipline them accordingly. For example, your five year old child should not be put in time out for 15 to 20 minutes. That is too long. The time out needs to be according to the child's age. A five year old child needs a time out of no more than 5 minutes, and a ten year old child requires a maximum of 10 minutes etc. It is of vital importance to make sure that all family members are on the same page when it comes to disciplining the child.

CHAPTER 6

Calming Your Child

Due to the sensitivity, of the sensory system, that exists in most of these children, many parents will tell you that the following techniques work extremely well for their children. The trick involves finding out what your child likes and dislikes. Once you find a technique that works for your child, use that technique to help calm them. Words of caution, these children become bored very easily so don't be surprised if the technique that works for this month, fails to work the next month.

- Pushing them in a swing.
- Putting them in a hammock.
- Using brushing techniques, like patting or brushing the child's skin while it is dry. This activity creates a calming effect and helps with blood circulation.
- Put them in a snoezelen room. A Snoezelen room is a relaxing environment with a focus on leisure. Relaxation is promoted through gentle stimulation of the senses: sight, smell, hearing, touch and movement. The child is not pressured into doing any activity; therefore, there is less tension on the autistic child.
- Some children like to sit in the car while it is in parked position with the windows up. They keep turning the steering wheel for a very long time. I believe the reason for this

behavior relates to the child feeling safe in this enclosed, cocoon-like space while at the same time experiencing control by turning the steering wheel without any interruption.

- Certain children like the sound of music. These children listen to soothing music set at the right volume. Our son possessed a keen ear for music and knew the right volume and base to tune in to.
- A number of children like pacing back and forth, or, spinning some type of object for hours without becoming bored.
- A nice warm bath helps certain autistic children stay calm. Be cautious about this activity. If you do not supervise the children regardless of their age, you can have a flood in your house.
- Riding horses provides an alternative therapy. Some parents let their autistic children take riding lessons, as they believe that this too provides a calming effect on their children,
- Give the children their favorite toy. One autistic child I met goes around all day listening to her favorite Christmas song and story on her IPAD. She carries on this activity even in the middle of July and you dare not take it away from her. If you remove it, the behavior sets in.
- Taking your child for a walk in the park creates distractions from the existing behaviors as she may even starts enjoying the change of scenery.
- You can purchase several different sensory products for your children to help keep them calm. Products such as weighted blankets and vests, portable weighted lap pad, mood and calming lights, and sensory pillows. Other products exist as new products arrive on the market regularly. The internet offers a great resource for finding these items.

- Swimming, or water therapy, proffers another useful activity. Teach your child to swim as it produces a calming effect as well.

As each child presents with different temperaments, you need to explore for a technique that suits your child. The list is not limited to the above. These just represent a few techniques that a variety of parents find useful to calm their children.

CHAPTER 7

Feeding Your Child

Feeding a child on the autism spectrum can be a struggle as most of them acquire unusual eating habits. Some crave foods that provide a crunchy texture. Certain children crave sugar; others crave spicy, bitter or sour foods. Some fail to eat any fruits or vegetables. Specific children love to eat fruits and vegetables, while still others will not eat any meat at all. However difficult this situation might be, it remains a major part of the equation in helping your ASD children.

No magic cure for PDD exists. The diagnosis includes Autism, ADHD, ADD or, even Schizophrenia and Bipolar disorders which evidence some similar symptoms. Despite these facts, we can all agree with one thing; all possess one thing in common, the condition called inflammation.

How can you tell when someone exhibits inflammation? Usually inflammation in the body presents with pain, heat swelling or redness. However, there is another type of inflammation that is called silent inflammation. This type is difficult to detect as no warning signs appear out wardly until the disease exhibits severe symptoms.

Most parents swear by their first born that once they removed inflammatory producing foods from their children's diet, the children react positively to the change in diet. The parents noticed huge improvements in the children's behavior, even though that does not cure autism.

Why do you think this change comes about?

According to Dr. David Perlmutter in his book, "Grain Brain," Autism retains features of an inflammatory disorder of the brain. Research documents show that autistic individuals acquire a higher level of inflammatory cytokines in their system.

What are *cytokines*? According to Ananya Mandal, MD, cytokines refer to cell signaling molecules that aid cell to cell communication in immune responses and stimulate the movement of cells towards sites of inflammation, infection and trauma.

What are some of the causes of inflammation? The basis of inflammation includes poor diet (such as sugar, trans-fats and processed food), lack of exercise, and stress. You might ask "What type of stress can a very, young child face?" Think about all the stressors in the environment that an autistic child copes with each day. These stressors include schools, an environment with a significant amount of tension, a setting which restricts what they want to do, an atmosphere of bullying, sibling rivalry, etc. Need I say anything more?

Inflammation arises from many different causes. Hidden allergens exist such as gluten and dairy. Hidden infections occur from viruses, parasites, yeast or bacteria. Toxins contribute to the inflammatory process such as mercury, paints, carpets, pesticides, molds, myco-toxins, black mold or building materials in homes or schools.

Therefore, if we possess the knowledge that feeding our children certain foods will cause an increase of inflammation in their systems, shouldn't parents be eliminating these foods, and replacing them with healthier food choices? Let's look at some of the ways we can offer our children healthier choices, plus provide them with an abundance of the nutrients required to help them with normal growth and development.

This situation is not a 'one size fits all' as each individual requires different approaches. Parents need to know their children and once possessing that knowledge, healthier choices using creative methods can be decided for them.

Healthy foods, like fruits and vegetables, become an issue. Little Billy tells you that he does not want to ingest fruits and vegetables because it tastes yucky. Don't tell him that it is okay, he can have something else. Eating lots of fruits and vegetables on a daily basis is a requirement for every child. I don't care how you do it. Just do it. I hear parents saying all the time "I just cannot get my child to eat fruits and vegetables," and I will say to them "get creative." Get it to them in smoothie or juices, put it in their favorite foods, bribe them, use the WIT method (whatever it takes) to get them to have fruits and vegetables on a daily basis. Even if you have to bribe them with their special treat, get them to eat these foods. You see, it is better to have them ingest the good stuff first, and then the junk food goes in after. When the child consumes enough of the good stuff, there will hardly be any room for junk food.

If at all possible feed them those fruits and vegetables in their natural form. What I mean is for you to plant your own garden or obtain organic food (no chemicals or pesticides) from a local farmer. Nowadays, organic foods get the big hype. This simply means foods that are grown naturally and without chemicals.

A multitude of different fruits and vegetables exist in the world. Don't you think there is a slight possibility that your child will take a liking to a few from the large variety available in nature? They do not need to have them all. Let's look at a few examples of fruits and vegetables and ways to prepare them.

Kale: This dark green leafy vegetable contains a rich source of iron, fiber, sulfur, vitamin K, vitamin A, vitamin C, calcium and antioxidants. Several ways exist for you to prepare this vegetable that your children should love. Some methods include adding it to smoothies, steaming it, making it into chips and using it in a salad or soup.

Spinach: Spinach represents another dark green vegetable that possesses iron and many other health benefits. No wonder most of us loved to watch the TV cartoon about Popeye the sailor man. Popeye would eat his can of spinach and pump up his muscles for us to see. This cartoon represented a great show for children to watch due to the influence exerted by television. One can steam this vegetable, add it to smoothies, make a juice out of it, make it into a salad and even put it into your soups or other dishes.

Carrot: The sweet taste of this vegetable allows it to be eaten raw and you can give this to your child as a snack. The carrot is rich in Beta-Carotene which provides a great benefit for the eyes. Of course, it can be steamed as a vegetable, placed in soups and stews, used as a snack, or, in a salad, made into a pleasant juice or, cooked with roast beef.

Cucumbers: The cucumber, like the carrot, makes great snacks. Cut up and put it in your child's lunch bags. Remember to eat it in front of your children. I mean really eat it so that they see you eating it. They might think to themselves: "Well, if mom and dad eat it, it might be really good for me".

Apples, pears, peaches, pineapples, oranges, strawberries, blueberries, bananas, raspberries, mangoes, grapes, apricots, gooseberries, guavas, and melons are just a few of the many fruits available. The list goes on and on. Children usually like certain fruits due to the sweet taste, but, need to get use to the texture of the fruits as well. You might find that your child will like a few of them, but if they don't, sneak it in their food.

You need to examine your child's diet. Note, what she craves and what you are feeding her. Keep a food diary of what the child is eating and what reaction occurs after consuming the food. I remember our son's manner as being very nice and calm before eating. Once he finished eating, he would be jumping all over the place. We joked around stating "Why did we feed him, he was nice and quiet before he ate?"

Get your child tested for any food allergies. Whether the allergen comes from wheat, casein, gluten, dairy or whatever the case might be, you want to eliminate those foods entirely from the diet if the child has allergic reaction after eating these foods.

Get the more active children involved in preparing the foods. They might want to participate more and to eat what they prepared instead of being instructed to eat food they do not like. Make it a fun experience for them.

Eliminate artificial sweeteners, processed and refined foods, preservatives, additives, sugars and dyes as much as possible from the diet. Home-made food provides one of the most nutritious diets, because you control what you put in the meal. Simplicity affords a great way to go. It offers a quick and easy method, and chances are you add fewer ingredients.

Sweeteners represent a main factor that possibly contributes to your child's behaviors. Sugar exemplifies one of the major sweeteners you want to avoid feeding your child. Why? Sugar is addictive. Have you ever tried eating something with a high sugar content only to find out that you are compelled to keep on eating and eating and wanting more?

Sugar comes concealed in many forms such as the breakfast cereals that your child loves so much. Even though, some brands contain the word healthy on the box and include fruits, check the sugar content, it might surprise you. Breakfast bars, yogurt, bread, real fruit juices, sauces, peanut butter, milk, and dried fruits just to name a few that are all high in sugar content.

You need to avoid giving your child the other sweetener, high fructose corn syrup. High fructose corn syrup is derived from corn that undergoes processing to convert some of its glucose into fructose. This process creates a very toxic substance. It appeared on the market in 1978 as an inexpensive alternative to table sugar in juices, sodas, candies and other food items. Other sweeteners that you should avoid include aspartame, agave nectar, and sucralose.

Try to eliminate these sweeteners from their diets, as much as possible. When shopping at the grocery stores, the trick entails reading the label of grocery items. As my teacher, Joshua Rosenthal said jokingly, "If it has more than one ingredient, or if you cannot pronounce the name of the ingredients, don't buy it."

In today's world, it remains crucial that you watch what you feed your family and yourself. In the past, less people existed in the world to feed and the demands for food stayed low. As the population increased, it put more pressure on the government to provide more food, and in the process, mass production occurred. Therefore, when feeding your family make healthier choices. I am not saying that this is the cause of autism. My point is that, you should make healthier choices because food can be medicine to some and poison to others. No one size diet fits all.

Give your child a good multi-vitamin each day to help form a balanced diet. You can obtain vitamins from the health food store, the pharmacy, a good nutritional company or, the grocery store to name a few places. If you do not know which one to buy, speak to your child's pediatrician or family doctor. In most cases, the health care provider will refer you to a good one that suits your child's needs.

Some people describe the vitamin industry as a big money making machine. I refrain from commenting on that at this time. My theory contends that, if you think that your child now breathes very clean air with no toxins, obtains all the necessary nutrients that they need from the food they consume, drinks clean unpolluted water and gets at least eight hours of uninterrupted sleep; then they might not need to supplement their diet. However, if you answer no to any of the above, you might consider providing them with a good multi-vitamin.

For the children that exhibit no nut allergies, incorporate more nuts into their diets, such as walnuts or almonds. These nuts provide nutrients to the brain. Have you ever noticed how the walnut is shaped like the brain? Raw cashews afford another good one as long as you feed it in moderation

Another key factor that we need to pay attention to is; to teach our children how to chew their food properly. Chewing adequately helps them digest the food much better. I remember as a child, my mom used to tell me to chew my food thirty two times. I failed to understand why at the time, however as I got older I started to comprehend the reasons why she told me to do so.

Beverages

Most children (not only those with autism) like drinking sugary beverages such as soda pops, concentrated juices and even juices in containers with '100% real fruit juice' labels. Just read the label and it will surprise you to see the amount of sugar content in that juice container labeled 100% real fruit juice. If you want to give your children juices, dilute the juices with equal parts of water, or, better yet, make your own home-made juice from scratch.

The best liquid to quench your child's thirst remains 'plain old water' of good quality. Our bodies consist of 80% water. Therefore; we need to pay attention to the amount of water that we are giving to our children. Some youngsters dislike drinking water due to the tasteless flavor.

Some ways exist to improve the taste of water and make it more palatable. Consider investing in a good water filtration system if possible. A lot of different systems appear on the market these days. Some brands even separate the acid from the water making it alkaline and as you and I know less disease live in a highly alkaline body.

Cut fruit slices such as apples, peaches, oranges, strawberries etc., and put in your water and refrigerate it. This mixture makes a pleasant tasting drink that the entire family can enjoy. I normally add a few slices of lemon to the water or, cinnamon stick and apple slices in different combination in the water. Experiment with different combinations. Get your child involved with choosing the fruits, or, putting water in the container so it becomes a fun activity that she is involved in.

A key factor to remember relates to communication with your child's teacher. When your child is in school, you must let the teacher know that the youngster might require more time than the average student to go to the washroom, due to drinking a lot of water. Since the child might not be able to communicate her needs and may act impulsively, the teacher or caregiver might think that the child displays behavior issues by constantly getting up out of her seat. Therefore, always notify the teacher or the caregiver about this essential information. You might also consider including this vital piece of information daily in her communication book.

Grains: You can incorporate whole grains in your child's meals such as brown rice, millet, kasha, bulgur, rye, quinoa, amaranth, barley, buckwheat, flaxseed, oats, organic corn, muesli, spelt and the list goes on and on, of course, these are just some of the most popular granular seeds. I know you must be thinking by now that you are not familiar with some of these names. Nonetheless, welcome to my world. I started where you are, then I started studying nutrition. I became familiar with these granular seeds, plus more, and learned the benefits of the whole grains.

Protein: Since protein provides the building blocks for the growth and development of your children, you want to feed your children protein. Amino acids, the smaller structures in protein, build muscle mass, help with healthy vision and facilitate the proper function of the immune system.

Quality sources of protein come from meat, fish, some vegetables (such as sprouts, garlic, dried seaweed, grape leaves, green peas, onions, some mushrooms, broccoli, kale, asparagus, collards, cauliflower and parsley) pure amino acid, eggs, cheese (if this can be tolerated), tofu, legumes, beans, yogurt, seeds and nuts. These represent just some of the most popular ones. As you can see, even if your child dislikes eating meat, she can still get plenty of protein from other sources. I remind you of the following key fact about protein and vitamin B12. If your child dislikes eating animal products and you feed her protein from other sources, provide her with vitamin B12 supplement since you can only get B12 from animal products.

Notice that the key element in all these processes requires the concept of balance. This critical concept compels the parents to feed their children a balanced diet on a daily basis. Sometimes, you will be unable to provide a balanced diet. For example, occasions arise like when you are travelling and not able to prepare home cooked meals. Therefore, you rely on fast food, or, food already prepared by someone else. As long as you feed your child healthy foods at least 80 to 90 percent of the time, you are doing okay. This allows room to 'cheat' when you can't prepare home cooked meals. These situations illustrate the chief reason to give your ASD children a good multi-vitamin. A reminder that balance remains the key point in everything you do.

CHAPTER 8

Keep Your Child Active

Children require some form of exercise to prevent boredom, to help them feel better, to burn off extra energy and to grow and develop normally. Remember when you finished an exercise class or participated in sports, how did you felt? Did you feel energized, or, did you focus better mentally? Do you think your child will experience the same results? It could be as simple as going for a hike in the woods for 15-20 minutes doing jumping jacks, or signing them up for a sport that they enjoy. Whatever activity you have them doing, they will thank you for that.

Words of caution: Make sure that the type of exercise you choose suits your child. Every child is different. For inactive children, obtain recommendations from your child's doctor for the best form of exercise for that child. Also, when some children on the spectrum reach a high level of exhaustion, they react by becoming more aggressive. Therefore, work with your children's doctor to determine the most suitable type of exercise for that child.

CHAPTER 9

Communicating With Your ASD Children

As parents, we understand our children more than anyone else. We seem to know what they want or what they are trying to say most of the time without them even uttering a word. This ability goes by the name of *maternal and paternal instinct*.

How do you communicate with the verbally expressive child? Note that even a child with high verbal skills, might exhibit problems communicating with others. We need to take their level of ability into consideration when verbally interacting with them and let others know about their capability.

One parent shared with me that she prepares a book about her child that she gives to any new caregivers or teachers. This epitomizes a marvelous idea. If a person has no idea about dealing with a child with autism, they can read the book and know all about her child. I recommend that the caregiver, or teacher, read through that book before interacting with a child that is on the autism spectrum. You might consider writing a few paragraphs about your child. It does not have to be lengthy.

Speak slowly to them and wait for them to respond. If they fail to answer right away, do not get frustrated. People interacting with these children must have a high degree of patience. While you wait for a response, the child might just be processing what you said to her. Also, they may not look you in the eye while speaking to you, as eye contact is very difficult for them to do.

At times communicating with them through pictures provides an alternative method of contact. Even though the child might be verbally expressive, this technique helps them to more effectively understand what you are saying.

Communicating with nonverbal children presents a trickier situation. You can sit on the floor to be at the same level while interacting with them. Sing to them. Ensure that it is a favorite or, well-liked song and repeat this over and over, several times per day until the child starts showing an interest. They may attempt a response by making sounds or moving their lips; sometimes they even elicit a chuckle. When this happens, express your excitement and document a note of their progress. If you see progress, continue this for a while longer to see how it goes. Discontinue once the child gets tired of that activity.

You can also play games with them to promote interaction, but these must be fun games that generate the children's interest. If the game is not stimulating and motivating, they become bored or lose interest.

Give toys that generate playful interaction. Toys can include their favorite TV or movie characters. In fact, using their favorite play thing initiates more interest in this activity and that in turn stimulates further learning.

Use pictures and gestures when speaking with them. For example; if your child picks up a cup, say the word cup to the child. Then put the cup to your mouth followed by placing it at the child's mouth; then pour a beverage of the child's liking in the cup, and repeat the activity.

Remember to speak to the child at their level, and use one, two or three word sentences at a time. Do not complicate the situation for the child, keep it simple.

When playing with your child, pay close attention to your child's behavioral actions. If the child picks up a ball, say the word, ball, slowly; then roll the ball to the child or throw the ball to them. Do this several times until the child tires or become bored with the game.

If a speech therapist works with your child, you will receive directions for exercises to do with your child in between the therapist's visits. Practice these exercises with your child on a regular basis. I know how tedious and arduous this is with everything else to do, but, both you and your child will benefit immensely from this in the long run.

Don't ever perceive that just because your children fail to speak that they lack the ability to hear and understand your verbalizations. I noticed my friend's son listening in on a conversation between his mother and I discussing him, and he suddenly got up and proceeded to cry. We registered shock at his behavioral response. Since this occurrence, I always make a point of not discussing my child in front of him unless I am including him in the discussion. Even if a child does not speak, they are very intelligent human beings. Most of them hear and understand what is being said. Therefore, refrain from speaking about your children in front of them and always remember to converse about positive matters to build up their self-confident.

When our son developed a meltdown, I imparted to him how much I love him and that he is a good child, but I firmly told him that I did not like that particular behavior. By directing him back to the behavior, we have alerted him about the unacceptable behavior, while at the same time letting him know that we still love him and that he is a good child. In this way, we showed him that we desire him to change his behavior.

Talking to your children about their diagnosis

When should you speak to your ASD children about their diagnosis? There is no set time or age. As parents, you will know when they are ready for this discussion.

You do not want to start too early as they might become confused about what you mean; likewise, you do not want to wait too long as they might become frustrated and angry. Depending on your child, you will know when a good time arises to start talking to them. I know this undertaking can be very unnerving as we avoid talking about it as much as possible with the child, but this task must be done at some time. You want to start by impressing upon them how special they are and that being special can be a grand thing. Give them a little information at a time to prevent overwhelming them. Tell them about famous people who were suspected of having autism. People like the following examples:

> **Daryl Hannah** - an actress;
>
> **Courtney Love** – a great musician;
>
> **David Byrne** - Oscar winner musician;
>
> **Tim Burton** - Film producer;
>
> **Bob Dylan** - *Legendary American Musician and artist;*
>
> **Bill Gates -** Businessman, programmer, former CEO and chairman of the world largest personal computer software company, and one of the world richest men;

Andy Warhol -American *Artist*, popularly known for his visual art movement;

Woody Allen – an American actor, director, screen writer, comedian and musician;

Michael Jackson - King of pop and an American singer;

Sir Isaac Newton - a very famous English physicist and mathematician; regarded as one of the world most influential scientist of all time;

Steven Spielberg - renowned American director and producer;

Abraham Lincoln - sixteenth president of the United State of America.

The list goes on and on, but your child will feel good when he realizes that these well-known people possessed these special gifts that they shared with the world. Also, they grasp that others share their same plight so they are not alone. The trick encompasses a way to find out what skills, or tasks, appear noticeable in the child's abilities and help them to work on that talent while boosting their confident and developing that expertise to perfection. Uncovering this ability could be one of the best things that you could do for your child as they all have very special hidden talents. Our job as parents is to help them to discover and develop those skills.

Talking to your ASD children about sex and relationship:

How do you go about talking to your children about sex and relationship and at what age? It is a good idea to start talking to your children about sex as soon as in their early teens, as their little bodies develop sexuality the same way other teenagers do. However, they need more guidance and coaching than regular teenagers due to their inability to talk about their feelings and what they are going through. You should start talking to them about sex prior to them developing an interest in sex and relationships. Talk to them about masturbating in private.

Teach them about boundaries.

Visit the library and get books on different types of relationships to initiate the discussion with your child. Explain the difference between brother and sister relationships, parent and child relationships, friendship relationships and intimacy relationships.

You might need to do a lot of role playing with your child in order for them to understand the concept of the different types of relationships. Social stories denote a great way to teach them as well. If you don't know how to write or do a social story, obtain the help of a professional to help you. Teachers and social workers afford proficiency in doing social stories.

For boys, a male can better explain relationships to them, and for girls, a female can describe it more effectively. However, if this is not feasible, then do the best you can and assume the role the best way you can.

Instructional videos exist out there that you can use with your child. Schools often teach sex education. However, your role is to make sure that your child receives education in this area.

Some parents worry that their child will grow up without a partner, however, some will and some won't. It is not for us to decide.

Pay attention to your child as their hormones start changing and guide them in the right direction. Puberty can be a challenging time. At times you will need to ask for help, either from a professional, or, from someone who has gone through that process before. The preferable choice is parents that have gone through that process before. Parents who raise kids along the autism spectrum should join support groups. The members of these groups provide a wealth of information, and most of them are more than willing to pass along this information to help others.

Explaining the Concept of death

Explaining death to a child can be a very difficult thing to do. When it is a close family member, a pet, or a friend, it is even more difficult explaining it to a child that has being diagnosed with ASD.

Depending on the age of the ASD child and their mental capacity, you can start by giving them very basic information. For example if the person was ill, you explain how much the person was hurting and that in death they no longer hurt! They went to Heaven (or whatever you want to tell them). Let them know that the person or pet outgrew there body and will eventually get a new one with no pain.

You might want to hire a grievance counsellor in order to help the child with the grieving process. These experts excel in this field and will be able to explain the process to your ASD child in a more effective way.

If your child can communicate, elicit their emotional state by asking questions about how they are feeling. If they are unable to communicate, this creates a more difficult situation to engage the child. Pay special attention to them, keep them connected to the process and speak to them about the situation in a kind way. Even, if they cannot respond, that does not mean that they cannot hear you. Some of them will understand. Even if it is only for a day or a week-end, take a family vacation to a fun place, if possible. This event provides a distraction for a little while.

I remember speaking to an individual diagnosed with autism and she chatted with me about her father's Alzheimer and heart attack, followed by his eventual death. I asked her how she felt when her father passed and she verbalized to me that she felt sad and happy, because she felt really sorry for her mom as her father was no longer there to keep her mother company. She went on to say that she really does miss her dad and wishes that he was still around; nevertheless, she feels happy to take care of her mom.

By showing the ASD child just a little bit more love, one can give them the assurance and security to know that another person still exist to care for them.

Explaining to your child about bullying

Children fear the unknown. A child without autism sees themselves different from an autistic child. Due to this different perception, the child without autism will sometimes tend to make fun of the autistic child or even act as a bully to that child. It becomes very difficult to teach a non-verbal child about bullying. However, a few methods exist to expose the child to the concept of bullying. You can watch movies on the subject of bullying with your child, do role play and social stories. Just do the best you can hoping that your child will get the concept somehow and if they don't, just do your best. You can only pray to God, the Universe, Allah, and Buddha or, whoever you believe in, that your child will be taken care of and not be deprived. Other children will take advantage of them, because they remain so naïve in nature. This explains one of the reasons that the nonverbal child will always need to have a special needs assistant or, a one to one person to help and protect them from these situations.

One family I interviewed described how at the age of 21, her son admitted to her his experience with bullying at a younger age in school. The other children used to laugh and make fun at him. He expressed an inability to know how to deal with the situation, or, even who to tell. He would act out his frustration in inappropriate behaviors so that he could get sent home from school. At home, he felt safe and no one would make fun of him. It must be noted that while he was at school, this child had a special needs assistant with him at all times and yet he still suffered bullying. When it was happening to him, he remained unable to talk about it.

How difficult can this be for our children? Due to the problem communicating their needs, these children suffer punishment in so many situations, even though they are only trying to express themselves.

CHAPTER 10

Celebrating Your Children's Birthdays

Planning birthday parties for your autistic children can be very problematic when 'no-shows' occur. Occasionally, regular children fail to want any association with a child that is on the spectrum. They prefer not to attend these birthday parties. The child that is on the spectrum can become very disappointed and feel let down.

You should always plan the birthday party around the child's main interests. Various ideas exist on how you can help your child enjoy her birthday and prevent them from becoming disappointed such as:

- Invite a selection of your friends with kids around the same age to the party. Invite extras to allow for no-shows.

Parents of autistic children report that, once other people realize that you have a child on the autism spectrum, contact is severed by some family members and friends. These friends and family members fail to show interest in understanding autism. They become fearful about interactions with your child and terminate the friendship and move elsewhere with their lives. A few of these people see your child as having a bad influence on their children or, maybe some of their children prefer not to be seen with an autistic child that they deem 'not cool'. Of course, the cause could very well be from peer pressure. Sometimes, it may be better that they are no-shows.

- Invite caring, loving, and understanding friends and family members who will help build your child's self-esteem.
- Sometimes, in place of throwing a party, take your child to an amusement park or some other favorite fun place for kids.
- You might contemplate taking them and the guests to the movies. Limit it to immediate household and or close family members. Even if you have a small family, it is still okay.
- If your child likes bowling, consider taking the child that is mobile, to a bowling alley. Your child will have fun and you both will be happy. Remember the rule of thumb: fun is required at a birthday party.
- Invite other individuals that are on the autism spectrum. Chances are that; they will be delighted to attend. In all probability, they will fail to appear on the invitation list of non-ASD kids' birthday parties.
- If they like going to the museum, this is another great option for an outing.
- Do family trips to the beach, the mountains or even the mall to celebrate the birthday.
- Plan a family outing to a restaurant of the child's likening.

Find something your child likes doing on that special day; after all, it is her day. You might be surprise with the ideas that your child might come up with, given a choice.

CHAPTER 11

Taking Your Child to Different Professionals

Dentist

You need to work with a dentist demonstrating expertise in working with children along the spectrum, because it takes a great deal of patience to work with these youngsters.

Speak to the dentist prior to the first visit and explain to him what you are doing to bring him on board with your plan of action.

Next, take the child to the dentist office perhaps several times before treatment, in order for him to become accustomed to the dentist, his staff, the surroundings and the apparatus that the dentist uses. At the first visit, your child might just shake hands with the dentist, his staff and sits in the dental examination chair. Some dentists indicate prior experiences with this process and will even describe other useful ways to familiarize the child with their procedures. Consider writing a social story about the entire procedure and read this to your child, before the first visit.

On the second visit you place the child in the dental chair, once again, get him to open his mouth and say "aaah" for the dentist. If you have an older child, you can use them to model for the ASD child what they are supposed to be doing. Chances are the child will do what their siblings do. If no sibling exists to role model, that is perfectly fine. You can initiate this process or use a method laid out by the experienced dentist that works for other kids and that might work for your child.

At the end of each visit, the dental office should provide a treat. You may need to bring in your own treat and just have the dentist or the staff give this to the child. For the most part, children want to keep going back just to get the treat, especially if it is their favorite treat. The dental office gives the treat at the end of the visit, so that the child realizes his favorite treat appears at the end of his appointment.

After two are three visits, the child should be ready for the first real appointment. The dental assistants and the receptionists usually assist in helping you organize this process.

Barber

Getting your child's haircut almost exactly mimics the same process as taking your child to the dentist. You need to obtain a hair dresser or barber possessing a lot of patience and demonstrating experience dealing with children with autism.

Start preparing the child way in advance for the entire experience; from the time you leave home until the end of the entire encounter. Write a social story and read it to your child several times. Once he arrives at the barber shop, have your youngster greet and shake hands with the barber and request the barber to give them a spin in the chair. The chair spin always provides a great treat for them and some barbers will give them a little loot bag once the hair cutting process finishes. This bag might contain a hair brush, comb or a special toy. This goodie bag provides a nice trick to entice them back to the next hair cutting session.

Blood work and your child

Taking blood from your ASD children, definitely entails a tedious job and most of them, hate being pricked with a needle and seeing their blood being drawn.

As with other experiences involving outside strangers, always prepare them in advance. Let them know what the entire procedure will be like. You can build a social story about the new adventure to the lab. Tell them how truly essential it is to have their blood taken. Do roll playing with them. For younger children, you can buy a toy doctor's kits and allow them to practice on a doll. Take turns practicing the simulated process until they get the concept. Thus, blood draws should occur without any fussing.

CHAPTER 12

Toilet Training:

Potty training can be a long drawn out process for some families, while others can complete it in a day. Some ASD kids grow into their teens and still fail to be toilet trained. All this depends on the functioning level the child is at and the ability of the parents or the caregivers.

So you asked, "What age should I start training my child to use the toilet/potty?" No special age exists to start training your child to use the toilet or the potty. You will usually instinctively know when the child is ready. Remember, passing urine in a potty, or the toilet, is a learned skill and you must teach them the same way you teach them all the other skills. Therefore, the earlier you start, the better and easier life becomes for you and everyone else, especially the child.

For those that are severely autistic, you might have to use a different approach. Some techniques are listed below that might be helpful:

Make it a fun event for your child. Turn the training into a party between just you and your child. You obtain the child's favorite treats. Every time that the child uses the toilet; you celebrate and offer her, her favorite treat.

Make fun out of it, clap and cheer, laugh, sing dance whatever works. Continue these fun activities until the child gets it.

You can involve a caring sibling in the process to show the child how to act appropriately in using the potty and then give the sibling a treat if the sibling is supportive and acts out his/her part.

If there are no siblings, you can demonstrate using the potty, and show the child what you are doing, followed by reinforcing "that is what I expect you to do." Be silly, do whatever it takes to get the child to get the message.

You can use social stories to help in this process depending on the functioning level of that child. Social stories aid in reinforcing the actual practice sessions.

Some parents stop using diapers on their children, replace it with underwear and let the children soil their clothes. The children then become uncomfortable and will want to use the toilet or the potty, if shown how.

You can also use books, tapes or videos to demonstrate the process to the child and hope that he or she gets the concept. You will need to repeat this several times to reinforce the learning. Just like all other learning, they will usually not get it on the first try.

CHAPTER 13

Teaching Your Autistic Teenagers about Self-Care?

How do you teach your ASD child about self-care? For a child that does not have a disability, it is much easier to teach them about self-care than a child that is autistic. It presents a huge challenge. Depending on the child, you start as soon as you think the child is ready.

You can start by teaching them personal hygiene. Show them the process of washing their hands before eating. Show them how to brush and floss their teeth after each meal.

Make it a fun experience, if possible. They learn better when the experience is interactive, pleasant and entertaining.

You can use videos, pictures, and once again, social stories. For high functioning autistic children, you can explain to them the reason why they need to brush their teeth, have a bath/shower etc. Explain to them what happens when one does not take the time to take care of personal hygiene.

Some people believe that when their child exhibits a disability that they have to do everything for them. Do not fall into this trap. You should be working with your child to get them to an independent state wherein they function on their own, as much as possible. This will enable them to live in the so-called real world.

This learning is such an important part of the journey with our children. While we are still here on this planet and capable, we as parents, need to focus our energy on helping our youngsters to be independent, so that when we are no longer here, they will be able to function without help as much as possible.

Parents, especially mothers, always want to protect their children. We worry about others taking advantage of them, we agonize about the future when we no longer exist. How will they cope? Do you think a better option would be to take that concern and refocus it on teaching them independent life skill; impart to them the basic skills for survival and independence?

I know how hard it is to see things in this way now, but trust me, your child will thank you when all is said and done. In the end, you will be much happier that you pursued this route.

I remember at times being very over-protective of my son; I would worry about him a lot and prevent him from growing up. Why? I needed to shelter him from the world. I put the blame on everyone except him for his inappropriate deeds. I did not let him take responsibility for his actions. What good did this do for him? I admit that it only crippled him. Maybe I was doing it for my own selfish reasons or maybe out of sheer love for him. Whatever the reason, I soon learned to let go of my fears and let the creator, God, and/or the universe handle the situation.

Social skills

Teaching your child how to act at home, at school and in the community at large becomes a vitally important issue. Imagine your child going to the mall and taking off every piece of her clothes as these children sometime do. They fail to care who stares at them. All they perceive is the need to get undressed. It does not matter where. By teaching them skills to become aware and knowledgeable about how to act outside of the house and in the community, they learn socially acceptable behaviors.

Parents of autistic children need to teach their children everything about social settings, to provide them with basic knowledge to be able to function in society. They cannot ill afford to take for granted, things that parents of regular children would do. Our children that are being diagnosed with autism, exhibit very unique personalities and need constant reminders.

Rest assured that you do not have to deliver all the education yourselves, as public and private organizations exist with one of their primary goals directed at teaching your child these skills. Just remember to ask for referrals and work in conjunction with the organization to obtain the best results for your child. You know your child best.

For higher functioning kids, a few skills that you need to work on with them include: answering the telephone, doing their own laundry, learning how to shop, washing the dishes, cleaning the house, cooking meals, managing money, securing the home for safety, acting safe in the community, acquiring the appropriate behavior for social settings, and discovering how to make friends. The list goes on and on; however; these provide you with a few examples.

Bath/shower

Some children prefer a bath over a shower and vice versa. Whatever they prefer, teach them to have a bath one to two times per day using the tools of social stories and role play to impart the information to them. Use visual aide and schedule boards to further get your message across to them. This instills in them when bath time is. The majority of these kids learn visually while others display both visual and auditory methods of learning. Use pictures to cue them to know when it is bath time or shower time.

Your goal should be to have your child become as independent as possible. Therefore, whatever method you use, you should be able to move them toward independence eventually.

Clothing

Some children like wearing the same clothing over and over again without removing it to be washed. If you happen to get the item removed from their bodies and washed, they will be happy to put it back on the minute it is clean. Get them involve in choosing their own clothes. Give them some control over dressing in what they want to wear. Get them involve in doing the laundry, tell them social stories about wearing clean clothing versus wearing dirty clothing. All these activities help increase their independence.

Your high functioning children would benefit from going shopping with you to shop for their own clothes. These children know exactly which clothes feel comfortable on their bodies. Some of them like wearing cotton material, whereas, others might like jersey fabric etc.

CHAPTER 14

Spiritual Practices

Spiritual practice of some kind helps your child to be well rounded. This religious activity helps develop their faith and leads to fostering a more respectable person. Take them to church, the mosque, and the temple, whatever your faith is. Usually, these organizations convene special classes for children. The children in these settings happen to be more receptive to autistic children than children in other social settings, because of their religious beliefs.

A great way of teaching your child about God and religion involves reading story books to them about these topics at bedtime or other available time. You can always borrow books from the library, or watch movies or videos with them about your faith. Books on tapes or in CD format also exist that talk about God. If your child likes singing, they will especially like listening to the songs about God.

CHAPTER 15

Self-injuries

Some autistic children become frustrated and take out their anger on themselves by inflicting pain on their bodies. Some bang their head against the wall. Others bite or scratch themselves or inflict other injuries.

We can help them by first trying to understand the reason for their self-injury behavior. Determine what they need. Are they in pain? Teach them how to communicate. It can be in sign language, in words, or in pictures etc. Again tell them social stories to teach them a better way of expression. Once they find a way to communicate their needs, they will use it and you will find that their inappropriate behaviors will decrease over time. It might take them a long time to learn that skill; however, once they learn it, it will be used with consistency.

As parents, it becomes very difficult to watch our children hurt themselves. If they cannot communicate their needs to us, and we are not able to understand their needs, it remains tough for us to help them.

Injury to other

Children with autism exhibit a high degree of sensitivity to feelings. It is amazing how they will run right up to someone in a crowd and hug that person; while they will go up to another person and just hit that person. It seems that they can pick up on other people's energy. If they feel positive energy, they gravitate to that person. If they feel negative energy, they walk right up to that person and start hitting the person perceived to be filled with negative energy.

Some children tend to be runners. When they are upset, they start to run. If you attempt to stop them by getting in their way, they will hit you, even if they did not mean to do so. They get frustrated and just want to run away to clear their minds. If the environment is safe, do not go after them. Let them run and clear their minds. They will return once they calm down. If you chase them, they will tend to run even further.

If the environment is not safe, you might have to bribe them just for their safety. Offer them something that they like. Speak to them in a kind, gentle manner. You must remember to stay calm, and not get upset, during the entire process, because they feed off your energy.

Once, calm settles in, discipline them in a kind and loving, but firm way. This happens to be a perfect time to tell them a social story or show them a video of what kind of accidents can happen when they run. Even though some of them might still not be able to understand, do it several more times. Keep reiterating and role playing the situation with them and hopefully one day they will comprehend.

Our autistic children also tend to take out their frustrations on the ones that love them the most, like their mother. I am not sure about the reason for this, but think about it. When you are frustrated, do you blame your mother for things that happen to you, even though it is not her fault? Well, this might be the same concept with our autistic children. The difference is that, they take it to the extreme which includes hitting. Of course, you would never think of hitting your mom when you are upset, right?

Preparing your child for changes and transitions:

Most children along the autism spectrum fail to do well with changes and transitions, and, will need help with this process to diminish inappropriate behaviors. I find that social stories and role playing represent great tools to use to help them during any change or transition.

You should prepare your children, as much as possible, when there are any changes in routine however; it becomes difficult at times because we do not have control over the given situation. When this happens, we must do our best to help them work through the changes and transitions by explaining to them that sometimes things will change, and that is okay. We should re-assure them that things will work out in the end, even with the change. By doing this, we will help them to reduce their anxiety level.

I was at the airport recently and saw a high function autistic lady traveling by herself. I had no idea as to where she was going but, it seemed that she had missed her flight and she was in frenzy. She was speaking to someone on the phone and proceeded to pass the phone to a complete stranger to carry on the conversation. She kept passing the telephone from one person to another until she finally gave the phone to an airline representative, who checked her boarding pass and confirmed to her that she had missed her flight. The autistic lady became flustered and overwhelmed; however, the airline representative was able to reassure her.

CHAPTER 16

The Teenage Years

So you have come this far caring for your child. He gained some really useful skills. When your child turns thirteen, then fourteen and even fifteen, you become really excited, thinking things are going to get much better, right? Wrong. This time period is when their hormones start acting up. Their little bodies are changing and they don't know how to handle it. They have difficulty explaining their feelings to you. Most of them do not have friends that they can speak to, because of their communication impairments. They start dealing with it the best way they know how with an increase in inappropriate behaviors. The majority of the parents that I conversed with, described that they saw an increase in their children's inappropriate behaviors once they turn 14 and 15 years old. Some parents said that the inappropriate behaviors became so destructive that they were forced to put their children in group homes (this will be a topic for later).

Some parents on the other hand reported that their children actually improved with age. These children received timely support and services as required. The parents had made sure that their children received services for behavior and communication issues. The youngsters had obtained immense supports from their families, communities and schools. Their parents actively took part in their well-being. These children will continue to thrive as long as they receive the supports that they need.

CHAPTER 17

Alternative Methods for Helping ASD Kids

Although little scientific proof exists for helping children with autism, some parents declared that they saw great improvement in their autistic children's behaviors after using specific therapies. Here are my thoughts on what happens. If you know that you have a problem eating or doing certain things, wouldn't you avoid eating or doing those things? Your symptoms will return however, if you go back to repeating the same things later on. Therefore, avoiding the foods that your children are allergic to will help to reduce some of the autistic traits and inappropriate behaviors.

The earlier the child receives a definitive autistic diagnosis, the better the chances of helping them improve.

This list itemizes a few of the alternatives that parents use to help their ASD children:

Biomedical therapy can include pharmaceutical modalities, but then again, most biomedical therapy is based on the Dan Protocol (Defeat Autism Now). So what is the DAN Protocol? According to an article written on about.com; the "DAN! Protocol," was founded by Dr. Bernard Rimland in 1960. The DAN doctors believe that autism is a biomedical disorder caused by lowered immune response, external toxins, vaccines and other sources, and problems caused by certain foods. Dr. Sidney Baker, one of the DAN doctors believes that diet and supplementation is one of the key factors for treatment of autism. Please visit website below for more details on this protocol.

(http://autism.about.com/od/alternativetreatmens/f/dandoc.htm).

Some autistic children benefit from special diets; and some parents believe that, by placing these youngsters on these specific diets will help to stabilize the children's behaviors. This makes perfect sense if you believe that we are what we eat. Have you ever noticed how, the minute you give them foods with high sugar content, that they start bouncing off the wall? Their negative activities increase and you say to yourself "Why did I feed them that?" On the other hand, if you feed them a diet with less sugar and starch you will notice the difference in their behaviors.

Although no one specific diet exists for individuals along the autism spectrum, some parents will tell you that they noticed significant changes in the children's abnormal behaviors when they put their children on a dairy and gluten free diet. Again one size does not fit all, especially for these children. What works for one might not work for another.

Vitamin Therapy; Some autistic children often benefit from vitamin B6 and magnesium. Vitamin B6, also known as pyridoxine, can be found in fish, meat and bananas. As an essential vitamin, B6 can only be obtained through the diet. Vitamin B6 provides nutrients for the health of every cell in the body and can only be obtained through diet and supplementation. Vitamin B6 is water soluble; therefore it cannot be stored in the body and must be reduced. B6 also is involved in making chemical that transmit signals in the brain.

Magnesium, a very important mineral in the body, can be found in many different food items such as green leafy vegetables, legumes, nuts, seeds, whole grains, some types of fish, beans and lentils, avocado, low-fat dairy products, bananas, dried fruits, dark chocolate, etc. Some parents supplement their children's diet with a combination of vitamin B6 and magnesium as an alternative therapy for autism.

Glutathione acts as an antioxidant in the body to combat molecules, called free radicals which damage the body's cells. Scientists believe that the levels of Glutathione, in autistic children, drop very low and by increasing that level, it miraculously helps these children with some of the symptoms of their autistic behaviors.

According to an article posted on insite.com by Michael Hunnman on August 15, 2011; 74 sicknesses and diseases, typically, are associated with low Glutathione levels. Autism is listed as one of them.

You can do a blood test to determine your child's level of Glutathione. The test is called a Live Blood Analysis Test, normal reading is greater than 669 micromol/L.

You might ask, what is glutathione? Glutathione is the body's master antioxidant. According to New Day Autism, a family support foundation, "glutathione is a very important protein made up of the three amino acids, cysteine, glutamic acid, and glycine. This protein is an antioxidant that is made in the liver and it protects body cells from free radicals."

The article goes on to state that since children with autism are deficient in glutathione, many studies have been done to test the effectiveness of the glutathione therapy. These studies have been published in medical journals and show that glutathione accelerators promise to replenish the supply in the body, when a deficiency of glutathione has been noted. As mentioned before, Live Blood Analysis test can verify the improvement after supplementation for a period of time.

Studies also revealed that children with autism possess a higher level of toxic heavy metals, such as mercury, lead, tin, bismuth, antimony, thallium, and tungsten in their system before treatment. These heavy metals are toxic and accumulate over time, especially in the brain. Heavy metals may be absorbed from the mother during pregnancy, or, ingested from toxins in the environment. Toxic metals show up in some fish, metal fillings in teeth, auto exhaust, lead, paint in old buildings, and cigarette smoke. If children have a deficiency in glutathione (the protein that binds to and excretes those toxins from the body as bile or urine) then it makes sense that their toxicity levels would remain higher than normal.

A newspaper article dated December 7, 2005 indicated that 287 toxins were detected in umbilical cord blood of new born; 180 cause cancer in humans or animals; 217 produce toxicity in the brain or nervous system; and, 208 cause birth defects or abnormal development in animals. Scientists refer to the presence of such toxins in the newborn as "body burden." For more information on this article, visit https://www.wsws.org/en/articles/2005/12/toxi-d07.html.

Children with autism and with a glutathione deficiency also present with a deficiency in Vitamin C and E, as glutathione is a necessary component for the proper absorption of these very important vitamins.

How do you increase your Glutathione level? There are several different ways to increase your glutathione level.

- Purchase it from a health food store and take it orally. The problem with oral ingestion is that; you do not receive all the benefits as it breaks down in your digestive tract before it reaches your blood stream, plus the GSH molecules is the wrong size and shape to enter the cell's mitochondrial which is where it does its work.

- Another way to boost your glutathione level is to take an ice cold bath. Think of all the discomfort this will cause your love ones.
- *Nutraceutical* companies exist on the market that sells supplements to help your body to create its own glutathione. They provide the pre-cursors to give your body the ability to create its own glutathione. Please visit pubmed.com for more information on Glutathione and autism.
- **Energy Therapy** elicits the energy in your body. This technique is a holistic healing method using one's energy: This energy is contained in and surrounding the human body, mind, and spirit.
- **Stem cell therapy** provides an effective and safe method of autism treatment and can help many children suffering from autistic spectrum disorder. Stem cell therapy addresses the issue at its core by initiating a repair process in the affected parts of the brain. However, cell therapy represents the dessert, not the main course. Integrated treatments including occupational therapy, speech therapy, psychological counseling, diet as the main course and educational program provides the most optimal results.
- **Hyperbaric Chamber** *(oxygen therapy) (HBOT)* utilizes a pressurized, oxygen-filled chamber or tube. It's an effective tool for treating the "bends" (a disorder among SCUBA divers who surface too quickly, causing oxygen bubbles in the bloodstream).

In recent years, some doctors theorized that HBOT could improve symptoms of autism by increasing oxygen intake and thus reduce inflammation and hypo-perfusion (lack of oxygen) in the brain. Of course, no agreement exists within the scientific community that inflammation or, lack of oxygen causes autism, or, is even generally associated with autism. However, some parents believe that at some time in their children's life, the children became deprived of oxygen whether it was at birth with the umbilical cord around their child's neck or some other time when a near drowning incident occurs. They will tell you that they think that oxygen deprivation could be one of the causes for their child having autism.

- *ABA (Applied Behavior Analysis)* is a reward based training technique that teaches your child new skills step by step. It has been known to be helpful in some children's behaviors. Each child presents differently with autism and it might not work for everyone.

- *Antipsychotic drugs:* Most psychiatrists prescribe different types of antipsychotic drugs for these children until they find one drug that works best for a particular child. It must be noted that the drugs alone will fail to work with the behavior problems. Other methods of behavior management must be used to effectively lower the negative behavior.

The drugs are being used as a calming agent to help the child to be calm enough in order for the other therapies to work. The medication purports to decrease anxiety and impulsivity in these children.

Words of caution; as parents, we know our children best and if your child is being prescribed a medication that actually increases the inappropriate behaviors in the child, you should report this to the doctor immediately. I have seen cases wherein children received medications that actually made the behaviors worse than they were before and the doctor had to stop the usage of that medication immediately.

- **Speech therapy** involves the treatment of speech and communication disorders and treats a very wide-range of conditions. A certified speech pathologist (sometimes called a therapist) must hold a master's degree. That person works in a private setting, a clinic, a school or an institution. They may also work as part of an educational team. They use a wide range of tools and interventions, ranging from toys and play-like therapy to formal tests and speech curricula.

- **Occupational therapy (OT):** According to the American Occupational Therapy Association, *occupational therapy is a skilled treat*ment used to help people to gain independence in all areas of their daily lives. OT's as they are usually called, assists people in developing the skills for the job of living necessary for independent and satisfying lives. Very often, you will find an OT working with injury victims to regain use of their hands. In the case of autism, (OT's) have vastly expanded the usual breadth of their job. In the past, for example, an occupational therapist might have worked with an autistic person to develop skills for handwriting, shirt buttoning, shoe tying, and so forth. But today occupational therapists that specialize in autism, may also be experts in sensory integration (difficulty with processing information through the senses), or may work with their clients on play skills, social skills and more.

- **Social skills therapy** incorporates the teaching of social situation skills. As autism spectrum disorders become more and more common, a sort of industry has grown up around teaching social skills to both children and adults. There is no such thing as an association of social skills therapists, nor is there an official certification in the field. Therefore, social skills practitioners come from a wide range of backgrounds and training which includes; social workers, psychologists, occupational therapists, parents, caregivers and speech/language therapists who have specialized in working with autistic individuals.

I believe that this represents a very important piece of the puzzle, as it remains very critical to have individuals along the autism spectrum become independent in order to function in this world.

- ***Physiotherapists,*** *(often called "PTs")* undergo training to work with people to build or rebuild strength, mobility and motor skills. Many physiotherapists hold a Master's Degree, or Doctorate, in physiotherapy, and worked in the field as an intern before working on their own. They must also be board certified by a national and/or state governing board. Individuals at the end of the spectrum can benefit significantly from a physiotherapist.

- ***Behavior Analysis*** represents a relatively new concept. It stems from the idea that behaviors, even when they are challenging or confusing, can be understood as a result of careful observation, record keeping, and analysis. Once behaviors are understood, they can be modified based on the needs and desires of the person whose behavior is at issue.

- ***Play therapy*** is a therapeutic approach which uses play as a tool for building skills in autistic children. Like Floor-time, it builds on children's own interests.

- ***Developmental therapy;*** teaches social skills. Because most autistic individuals find it difficult to develop social skills and display a hard time expressing their feelings and thinking abstractly, developmental therapies like Floor-time, Sonrise or RDI help them build these skills. To find out more about these tools, do a google search.

- **Visual based therapy;** uses pictures or videos. Most individuals with autism use visual methods of thinking. Some will do very well with picture exchange programs, such as video games, video modelling, or, other electronic communication systems.
- **Handle approach;** manages neurodevelopmental irregularities with a simple, non-invasive, empowering, and non-drug method. This approach is designed to enhance neurological systems that are causing learning or life difficulties.

It must be noted that some of the above have no scientific evidence; however, some parents insists that these therapies works well for their autistic children.

The earlier you receive a diagnosis of autism for your child, the earlier you can start helping her, and the more chances she will have to live a happier and fulfilling life.

CHAPTER 18

Education

Many parents indicate difficulty with locating proper education for their autistic children, whereas, other parents that have children with mobility issues, may not have any difficulty.

For parents of autistic children, one of the major problems involves children with a lack in the ability to communicate their needs. It can be very challenging with children that cannot communicate their needs to their teachers. Instead, these children act out their desires in inappropriate behaviors caused by fear and frustration that, they will not be understood by others. The child could be wearing a piece of clothing that itches but fails to communicate this to their teachers. The child may not be able to sit still because of her need for constant movement. The child could be bored because she fails to comprehend what the teacher is saying. Also, it could be problem with an upset stomach, hunger, etc. If the teacher fails to understand the child, and, if the child fails to understand the teacher, in that process, the child may receive punishment for her inappropriate behavior and get sent home or suspended from school.

The parents receive punishment as well, because in most cases they leave their jobs and rush home in a panic to take care of their children, or, having to arrange alternate care for the children. Sometimes, it simply is not that easy to find alternate care for children along the autism spectrum.

For a child that has a nanny, it is okay; however, not everyone can afford a nanny. Even with having a nanny, it still remains stressful for parents, knowing that the child is not able to be in school. In some cases, they change nannies on a regular basis due to burnout of the caregiver. Families with good support in place, from their family members and friends, find it easier, but, parents express concerns as to why their children cannot stay in school like other children.

One parent I spoke with told me that she developed a phobia. Every time her telephone rang, she developed a panic attack thinking that it was the teacher that was calling her to pick up her child from school. I asked her how many times per week she received these calls. She said depending on the week, she received a phone call anywhere between 2-4 times per week. Another parent shared with me that she could not dare to answer her home telephone and she let her messages back up on her answering machine so that the teachers could not leave her any messages. You might consider this irresponsible behavior on the part of the parent; however, you have to put yourself in that parent's position to judge her. Another parent described developing a phobia to schools and schools vehicles. Each time she sees a school or a school bus, she panics. When I asked her why, she informed me that it was based on all the difficult school meetings that she attended for her child, she just could not take it anymore and was progressing toward a mental breakdown.

Home Schooling

Some parents choose the option of home schooling their children and describe great success with this method. One of the reasons for satisfaction with home schooling is that; the children do not have to contend with outside stressors such as: children bullying them, teachers not understanding them, protracted sitting for long period of time in a classroom without movement, having to deal with crowded corridors, or spending long hours on a school bus before finally getting to a classroom. When you think about it, a lot of stimulus for a child along the spectrum occurs outside of the home.

By not having to deal with these extra, external forces, the child learns in the comfort of his home, develops more confidence and focuses on learning the curriculum. The drawback to this situation is that the parents end up spending more time with the kids without a break. If a way exists to obtain outside help during the day this could help out tremendously. I know some schools send in a teacher into the homes a few hours per week to help teach the children; however, this might not be enough. If so, parents would need to hire trained staff to help with home schooling, as well.

While home schooling, the children cannot stay at home all day, the parents will need to arrange different outings, such as going to the library to interact with other parents and home schooled kids, attending play groups, hiking, organizing and planning trips to the city, to the zoos, to different games, and to social skill classes, etc. If I had to do it all over again, I would definitely choose home schooling versus putting my child and myself through the many stressors that we have gone through.

Homework

Getting your child to complete their homework can be a challenge on top of everything else that needs to be done at home. One of the reasons that the homework is problematic is that, it might not be of interest to the child. The parents may be compelling them to complete it and the child becomes frustrated. Think about your own days in school. You might have expressed a great interest in mathematics, but not science and your parents and teachers forced you to take science in order to pass the grade. How did that make you feel? Did it make you sick to the point that you became stressed?

I think it is much better to capitalize on our children's interests and work with them to develop those interests to perfection. That way they can become successful, develop confidence, and feel good about themselves. However, those are just my thoughts, and, the homework must be done. So let's brainstorm some strategies as how to make it a fun experience for them. That way they will come to like and develop a keen interest in doing the homework.

The first thing that you need to do is discuss with your child's teacher how the work is to be done (what method she uses to arrive at the answers), as you might do it one way with your child, but the teacher, does it another way. By talking to your child's teacher about the method used, everyone will be on the same page. I remember showing our son how to do algebra one way and the teacher would show him another way. My son would get totally frustrated and I could not understand why he was getting frustrated. It was not until I met the teacher at the school conference that I became enlightened as to why our son was confused. Therefore, I ask that you communicate with your child's teacher about their ways of teaching to avoid frustration for your child and yourself.

Make it a fun experience for them. Don't have them start the homework as soon as they arrive home from school. You might want to give them a snack first. If they communicate verbally talk to them about how their day went at school or any other subject of your liking. For the ones that communicate non-verbally, after giving them their snack, you might want to have them play by themselves for about 15 to 20 minutes or, better yet, let them settle for some quiet time. Make sure you tell them that homework will start within a certain period of time, example in 30 minutes. I find that using a timer helps greatly, because it provides them with the visual aspect of time.

Make sure that the work is carried out in a quiet area of the house with less distraction. While you still have their attention, start them off with the most difficult assignment first. Depending on their attention span, give them one to two breaks in between. Be sure to provide them with a healthy snack on one of the breaks. A fun activity at the end of the work should be planned. This will be the motivator to finish the homework. What I find is that the child desires to get the work done as soon as possible, in order to get to the fun activity. Activities could include a trip to the library, baking cookies, going to the park, anything that they like doing.

I hope that this is helpful or, you might have your own method of getting your children to do their homework, but for the parents that do not, I hope that these suggestions help.

Individualize Education Plan

Individualize Education Plan, or, otherwise known as IEP are required for special needs students. All special needs students, identified with learning disabilities are entitled to a formal plan that describes how their schools will support their educational needs. This document can be challenging as some parents have no clue as to what this document means and how they should be completing it.

My advice to you is do research, read up on IEPs, and decide how it should benefit your child. If you still need more information after your research, you should go over the document with your child's teacher. Whatever you fail to understand, ask the teacher for an explanation. You can also get an advocate to attend this meeting with you, someone who knows the educational laws of your state or province. You could ask a parent who has gone through the same process that you are going through, or, obtain a paid professional.

The same goes for suspension documents. When it comes to these documents, most parents do not know their children's rights and should be seeking professional advice to help them with these educational issues. Advocates exist that you can seek out to help you with the process.

Parents possess a right to information in the School Record. Did you know that you have a right to ask for a copy of your child's school record and can request what documents stay in the file and what items should be taken out? Most parents do not have a clue about their rights and their children's school records. It might just surprise you to find out what information is being kept in these school files on your children, especially our ASD kids.

Meetings

If you are not comfortable attending meetings about your child by yourself, it is your right to bring a knowledgeable advocate to attend with you, as these meetings can be very challenging and disconcerting. For instance, you worry about making the right decision for your child. You want to make sure that you are signing the proper documents. You also want to provide the schools and agencies appropriate information about your child, but do not want information in the files that would prejudice the child later on in life. When the schools or the doctors offer your children medication for inappropriate behavior issues, you need to be informed as to why you should or should not accept their recommendations. These tasks can be very difficult as you are not trained in this area, thus, you need to learn a tremendous amount of information. You just hope that you are making the right decision. You can become very stressed with information overload.

Word of advice: When attending meetings about your child, it is wise to not have your child sit in on the meeting and hear negative comments being made about them. This can be quite disturbing for your child as they will lose self-confidence. School meetings, where there can be a lot of unconscious negative comments about the child is a good example. One needs to consider the child's feeling while sitting in on these meetings. In the long run, their exposure to such negative comments can be quite damaging to them.

If the child must be at the meeting, have them stay in a different room, maybe a supervised play room until it is time for them to attend and meet the participant of the meeting. You must make sure no negative comments arise at the time your child sits in the meeting.

We want to always promote positive experiences, as much as possible, for our ASD kids, in order that their self-confidence increases over time.

CHAPTER 19

Services For Autistic Children

Different government agencies approve a number of services for children with autism in various countries, states and provinces; however, these services are not readily accessible to the public on how to access these services. The internet remains a great resource to provide you with information on how to find and access these services. Otherwise, you can ask a member of the team that you created for your child to help you with this process. A team member should gladly help you access these services, or, at least provide you with the information on how to go about accessing the services.

Some of these services cut off once the child reaches eighteen, so the earlier you find out about and access these services; the better it will be for your child. Once they turn eighteen, not many services exist out there for them.

CHAPTER 20

Summer Camps

Summer has arrived and your autistic children, who are not being home-schooled are all out of school. What do you do with them? Do you keep them at home or, do you send them to camps and summer schools? Many specialized summer camps exist, that cater to ASD children's needs, whereas schools boards and private camps also exist to meet these ASD children needs. The trick is to find one that matches your specific child. Your child might like, sports, arts and crafts, drama etc. As no two children exhibit the same characteristics, it is best to register them for the camp that you think that they will enjoy the most.

Some of our children will need a support worker to accompany them to the camp. You can send your own support workers with them. When you select a camp, it is crucial that you give as much information as possible about your child to the team. This information help the staff to prepare for your child's needs.

Some parents choose regular camps, in order for their child to have additional experience of mixing and socializing with kids without a disability. It could go one of two ways; either the child will enjoy the regular children and learn from them, or, they will not like it and never want to go back. You might even have to retrieve them before the camp is over. If the experience ends as a failure with your child coming home early, the situation is still fine, as you will be able to cross that off your list of things to do the following year.

For residential camps, where the children stay anywhere from a week-end or more, this situation can be very tricky especially the first time your autistic child attends. The child will miss family members and home for a while, but eventually he learns to adjust with the help of the staff and other children. It is extremely helpful if the camp staff receive information about your child's needs. The staff and the other campers represent the key factors in your child enjoying his time at the camp. If they accept and treat your child well, your child will be more receptive and want to stay at the camp, because he feels happy, content and comfortable. Believe me, this event can build confidence and create a big difference in your child's life.

You, the parents, will be hurting once your children leave home. You will be torn between letting them go off to camp, and wanting to keep them at home safe and sound where you can see and care for them. But let me ask you this one question. What do you hope to accomplish by keeping them at home and not letting them go? You see by letting them go, you both are growing. Your child will learn new skills and independence, and you, the parents, learn to let go and allow them to grow. At the same time, you will feel contentment that you allowed them to experience the joys of camping and interacting with other children. This event could be the start of a whole new experience for your children that could teach them independence and open the doors to other life enhancing encounters outside the home.

CHAPTER 21

Finding the Right Caregivers

Looking for the right caregiver can be quite nerve wrecking and challenging for parents, especially mothers who do not trust anyone to look after their children. A lot of professional staffing agencies exist that will provide loving and caring services for your children. Do your in depth research and ask for referrals. Remember you know your child better than the less knowledgeable paid caregivers. Provide them with as much information as possible about your children. As mentioned earlier, I recommend having a hand book about your children with all the pertinent information about their specific needs. Talk about the triggers, dislikes, likes, what they like to eat or do not like to eat, etc. Provide any information that will give insight for the caregivers to understand your children, and be sure that, the caregivers read the handbook before they start caring for your children. Ask them questions from the book, in that case you will know if they read it. If not, look for another caregiver.

When an autistic child bonds with a caregiver, it can make a world of difference to the child's upbringing. The child will trust the caregiver, listen to, and follow the caregiver's instructions. Sometimes that's all it takes to correct some of the child's behavior. However, on the other hand, if the child does not like the care giver, they might not be compatible and this creates difficulty for both individuals.

Have you ever wondered how some individuals are able to work well with some autistic children, while others are not? It is like any other profession, some people are good at what they do; while, others just work for the pay check.

CHAPTER 22

Housing

Housing represents something that is very hard to think about; however, it exists as a reality. As a matter of fact, I remember one school principal suggested that we put our child on a waiting list for a group home. I remember being quite offended. Not my child. How dare she even mention this to us? However, there came a time when we really needed one and it created such a struggle for us to move in that direction.

Some children develop challenging behaviors during the teenage years between the age of 14 and 21, and you might not be able to keep them at home. A group home becomes a realistic option for them, and I can hear some of you saying that I must be crazy to even mention this. Trust me on this, I said the same words before, therefore, I can identify with you. The waiting lists for group homes remain extremely long, since there is a shortage of these homes, as more and more children are now receiving the diagnosis of autism. Therefore, put your child's name on a waiting list for a group home, and if you do not require the space, you can always turn it down later.

As I am writing this book, an article appeared that I saw recently; wherein, a 40 year old mother killed her 16 year old autistic son, and then killed herself. She left a note on Facebook stating that she was crumbling under the pressure of parenting her special needs son. She hoped that the government does something to rectify the problem. I know of one family who had to give up their child to the Children Aid Society to provide for safety for the child. Just imagine giving up your child to an agency just to save her life? Many other challenges and traumas exist that parents go through, but are too numerous to mention at this time.

Some children even ended up in **mental institutions**, because people around the autistic children misunderstood their behavior. The individual can spend several years in a mental institution without being able to get out of there. This situation can be devastating to both the children and their families. Imagine, a child growing up in the family home and all of a sudden he gets taken away from the security of his home, because of his autistic behaviors. The child gets placed in a mental institution and sometimes in a mental institution that is operated like a jail, amongst criminal convicts. The child gets treated like a convict even though no charges are filed for any criminal offences. This situation happens just because not enough placements exist for these children in proper facilities. Sometimes the children spend several years locked away in these institutions, how tragic for everyone.

This environment would be extremely difficult for these children, as it would not help an autistic child to recover. Certain people say that it is safer for the child and all other close individuals involved with the child. While in a secure institution, the child is considered to be safe because they would not be able to hurt themselves. Also, while in the confined environment, it would be safe for others, because the child would not be able to hurt others.

Let's examine the pros and con of this situation of incarceration of autistic children:

Safety for the child: yes, I agree that the child will be safe from physically hurting anyone including themselves. What about the psychological factors? How is this situation making the child better? I will touch briefly upon a few of the cons.

Social aspect: Since one of the deficiencies of autistic individuals is social impairment, locking them away in these institutions does not help, and only makes the situation worse, as no interaction occurs with peers to provide a positive influence. Sometimes, when these individuals act out with inappropriate behavior incidents, they remain in isolation for days without interaction with anyone.

When they come out of isolation, they re-integrated with other patients that are in these institutions. The autistic individual placed in the wrong setting ends up learning inappropriate behaviors as they adapt to their surroundings. Examples of inappropriate behavior could be that; they start using profane language that they never used before, or, making inappropriate sounds picked up from others etc. By the time they are ready to be back in the community, they will habitually use all those inappropriate behaviors that they learned in that environment and it creates another challenge to help them unlearn these unacceptable behaviors and to be integrated back into society.

The child tries very hard to control inappropriate behaviors learned in the controlled environment. When they make a mistake, they receive punishment for the inappropriate behavior, which can make matters worse. These children possess a disability just like any other disability. When a blind person can't see or a deaf person can't hear, what do you do to them? Do you punish them because they can't see or hear? Well the same thing occurs with someone having autism. One of the traits of an autistic individual happens to be deficiencies in communication. Inappropriate behavior is the best way they know how to communicate their needs, so you punish them because they cannot 'handle' their behaviors? Or, do you find better ways of helping them to cope and deal with the behaviors? How about teaching them skills to deal with the behaviors? How about teaching them coping mechanisms? That sounds like the most favorable way to me. What do you think?

One parent shared with me that she was promised that her child would obtain all the programs needed to help him to integrate back into the community. Three years passed by and her autistic child still remained in a mental institution behind bars with no idea when that child would be back in the community. Technically, the child received no schooling for three years while in that environment.

This mother was not even allowed to phone the institution to speak with her child. She could visit, but it is a 2-1/2 hour from home and she does not have a driver's license. When she did visit, she often received treatment like a common criminal, wherein, she had to go through a metal detector where even a bag of food was scanned by the institution staff to see what's in the bag. She said the experience is like going through the airport scanners. The child can call the mother, but when the child calls, she may not even be at home as she has outside commitments. It was recommended that she give the child her cell phone number. However; the child only remembers to call the mother on the home line as that number is stuck in his head being an autistic individual. She went on to relay to me that the doctors told her that the child will not be released until another agency takes this child. This statement means that the child will not be released to the family.

Such a decision affects the entire family. They have to spend unnecessary resources to commute back and forth to these institutions on a regular basis to visit their children. I must point out that in most of these situations, the children are been placed miles and miles away from home.

The families work. If you look at it this way, most of us work five days per week and get the weekend off. One day, the parents spend commuting to see their children and the other is spent preparing for work. Some only get one day off work and that one day they use for commuting to see the children. This situation can be very stressful, tiring and frustrating, especially given the fact that they have to see their love ones locked away and nothing can be done to help them.

More words of advice: Do everything you possible can to keep your child out of these institutions. If this fails to work and your child has to be placed in one, the trick requires thinking that things could always be worse. To keep your sanity, just be grateful for today, knowing that you may only have today and you don't know what tomorrow holds. The best advice for you, the parent, and family members entails obtaining lots of self-care which will be discussed in another chapter.

You must note that, not all bad things happen. Some of our autistic children graduate at the age of eighteen or twenty one and move on to become productive members of society. Some even write books and become role models for other autistic kids. I can think of one such individual named Donna Williams, her book is called "Nobody Nowhere." Some of our kids will continue to be dependent on their families for support for the rest of their lives. Whatever the circumstances, they will need our love and support. The best comforting words that I can leave with you is that; rest assured that the universe will continue to provide and take care of our children's needs.

Treatment Centers

Treatment Centers usually remain properly equipped to handle our children. They employ a variety of professionals on staff readily available to help our children.

Some will even use a more holistic approach using diets, spirituality and other therapies. They provide a school component that is built into the program as well. This environment is not meant to be a full time placement. Depending on the individual, they can stay anywhere from thirty days to as long as it takes to help these children change their behaviors.

CHAPTER 23

How the Diagnosis Affect Other Family Members

Some parents **separate or divorce**, with one parent failing to be able to deal with the situation. This leaves the other parent to deal with the child and other burdens and responsibilities of caring for the family which is very devastating to that parent.

The parent left behind will have to compensate for the departing parent. It is like a rug being pulled out from under your feet and if no support system exists, it makes it even worse.

This situation affects the children as well. They normally relate to two parents and now they have one. Think about a regular child without special needs when the family is going through a separation. This separation affects the child a lot and some even start eliciting emotional and psychological problems.

Now think back to a special needs child that cannot communicate, or, has difficulty communicating his or her needs. What do you think is going on in that child's head? We might think that they fail to understand. However, most of them do comprehend the situation and this fact can frequently cause them to regress or even end up with an increase in inappropriate behaviors. The parent left behind will usually be very busy trying to cope with the situation, looking after the autistic child and other family members, dealing with the emotions of separation and trying to find time for self-care. Again, self-care will be discussed later on in another chapter.

Dealing with all these issues, the parent left behind does not possess time to think about the reason the child's inappropriate behaviors escalated. They neglect to look after themselves in the process and this later causes a whole lot more problems in life.

One male parent described to me his worst nightmare. He states that when he takes his 11 year old daughter out and he needs to take her to the washroom, he cannot take her into the female washroom,, or the male washroom. Thank God family washrooms now exist in most public areas. However, for the places without family washrooms, this situation can be very awkward. He also shared with me his concern about when she turns 13 or 14 and starts having her periods. He is not quite sure how he is going to handle this.

So, what are the reasons why the family ended in separation at the precise time when they should be staying together during such a critical stage in life? Government fails to provide some services for autistic children that in turn create financial burdens for some families. Families find themselves in financial debt when trying to pay for these services for their children. The situation can become incredibly dramatic as sometimes the parents end up fighting and decide to go their separate ways. It is said that in a regular family, sometimes an extra $300 per month would keep families from the burdens of financial debt. Now think about a family with a special needs child that has to pay for all these additional services; what do you think the chances are of them getting into financial debts, which causes further problems in the relationship?

Neglect is another issue. One parent might feel that the other person fails to spend enough time with them, or is not paying them enough attention. Before you know it, they end up being separated or divorced before trying to sort things out. Sometimes, all that is needed on both sides is a little more understanding of what the other parent is going through. According to an article on CNN Health, 80 percent of marriages with at least one autistic child end up in divorce. This number might be higher as not everyone likes to admit that they have been divorced. Now think about a family with two or more children along the spectrum, what do you think the odds are? It is likely doubled.

Siblings:

Most frequently, siblings become jealous and resentful as the parents (mostly the mother), give most of their attention to the child with the autism diagnosis. This situation occurs because the parents feel guilty and try their best to compensate. Sometimes, they even over-compensate by trying to get that child back to a normal state. Trying to get the child back to a normal state means, trying to get the autistic child to fit inside a box, hypothetically speaking. Instead the parents should be allowing the child to be who he is and let them develop their special skills instead of worrying about the skills that they lack. In my case, I gave so much attention to our autistic child and sometimes forgetting about his siblings. I hope that they did not became jealous. If they did I can't say that I blame them. Had I been in their shoes, I would have felt the same way. You see no manual existed for caring for an autistic child or any child in particular, that says when this happens, do this, or when that happens, do that. You have to figure it out all on your own, and in the process, mistakes happen. You learn as you go along making up the rules as you go.

When I went grocery shopping, I normally focus on the reeds of our autistic child and what he required. Everyone else's requirements ended up secondary; this viewpoint yielded a bad move. When in reality we needed to create a balance and get everyone caring and sharing in the responsibility.

A sibling I interviewed said that dealing with the different agencies and school meetings cut into their family times. She explained that most of their time resulted in dealing with autism issues or advocating for her sibling. Therefore, time together doing fun stuff became very limited.

She remembered at one time her brother was suspended from school, her mom and dad had to work to provide for the family and could not afford to take time off from work that day. They did not have money to hire a baby sitter. Since she was attending university at the time, she ended up taking her brother to her class. Her brother behaved well and sat through her lecture a couple of times. The professor asked, why was her brother sitting in the class and not attending his school? She ended up explaining to the professor the reason he was there. The professor professed disbelief that this child who could sit through a university lecture was unable to sit in his own class room. What was the issue? What could be done differently in the child's class room to accommodate the child?

She described the situation bringing the family much closer together. She became very protective of her brother due to his disability and all the challenges he had to overcome. She further elucidated how very grateful she is now being older that she lived through the role of a sibling to a special needs child. Now, she can share experiences and speak to other siblings that are going through similar circumstances.

Sometimes, the older siblings will end up leaving home earlier than usual as they feel uncomfortable with the high stress level in the home and they just want to get away as far as possible from the situation. The special needs child again loses another family member and may elicit more inappropriate behaviors, because the absence of the sibling that they have known for a very long time creates a disrupting change in their lives.

Relative

When an autistic child is diagnosed in a family, one of the first things that you might notice is that the invitations to family gatherings stop. Sometimes, the parents become so busy looking after the child that they don't even become aware of this immediately. Why does this happen? Autism means a mental disability. Since autism exhibits no signs of physical disability, some relatives fail to understand autism and point fingers at the parents declaring that the parents do not know how to discipline the child and that explains why the child is like that. Please understand with these relatives, they mean well, they just fail to understand the diagnosis. You can help your relatives by providing them with information about autism. Send them information about this topic in the form of articles, books, videos, clippings, etc. and hope that eventually they understand autism.

In my family's situation, some of our relatives labeled us as bad parents; sometimes they even told us that the reason that we had an autistic child related to conceiving in my thirties, thus, being older. Or, some would say that we spoiled the child by giving him everything he wanted and that we never disciplined him. When my son was born, I was in my mid-thirties so these comments were quite painful for me. At that time I was looking for support from our relatives; but instead, they casted blame and shame on us. Fortunately, they gradually became more understanding as they came to be more knowledgeable about autism and would even send us newspaper articles on autism. We can now have open discussion about the subject. The shame and the blame are now slowly going away.

CHAPTER 24

Rewards

While parenting a child living with autism can be very challenging, it can also be very rewarding at the same time. However, most of the times we tend to focus on the challenges and often miss the rewards. Let's examine some rewards that you might receive while caring for your ASD children.

Appreciation

You learn how to appreciate the things that matter the most and to take nothing for granted. For example every time your child, has a good day at school, use the toilet for the first time, or say mama (for those that are usually not vocal), you express happiness and thankfulness. Each positive instance is like experiencing a miracle. Other parents look for their children to get good grades in school. You just want your child not to be suspended from school and to have a good day.

You learn to see things from a different point of view. Instead of saying: 'Why me Lord, why my child?' In time, you learn to say; "Now I know why I have a special needs child, and this is why this happens and that happens". It is just amazing how we adapt over time to situations once we get accustomed to it and see it from a different perspective that it is not all that bad.

Become better advocates

We become great advocates for children with autism. It can be very challenging to get services for our children. Over time, we become great at advocating for them, and navigating the different systems. In the process, we mature into experts. For the parents who are introverts, they soon learn to become extroverts.

I always like to use the analogy of the hen and the chickens, wherein the mother hen will do whatever it takes to protect her little chickens from danger. When the occasions arise, we do the same for our children. Then, when we have time to look back, we surprise ourselves and say darn; "Where did that come from?"

Develop patience

We acquire patience in the process of caring for autistic children, as most of these children exhibit lots of needs and you must be very patient with them. Take for instance; a child that has severe autism, he cannot speak and is not toilet trained. The only way of communication for this child comes by acting out behaviors or pointing. If the child feels pain, he starts to yell, scream or even hit just to communicate his needs. You become frustrated not knowing what to do. You already tried feeding the child, or, putting him to sleep, but the child kept on crying. Then suddenly, you decided to hug that child and gently massage the back. The child suddenly stops crying and voila!

You feel a sense of relief. You not only just learned patience, but you also learned to analyze your child's behavior. The next time the child cries similarly you know exactly what techniques work best for that situation.

Finding your path:

Some parents, or family members, will find their chosen career during the process of caring for their ASD family members. In one family, the sibling found her career path while she was in university. Due to all the different meetings and struggles that the parents faced with the schools and the school boards, the sister of an autistic child decided that she was going to become an educational lawyer to help families in need of help, with policies and procedures, plus laws for the education of children with autism. Some parents find their own career path. The principal thing is awareness and readiness to seize the opportunities, in the moment.

Gratitude

You learn how to be appreciative of the things that matter the most, and, to take nothing for granted. When your child sits still for a few minutes, you will be grateful; when the child graduates from one class to another you will be grateful, even if she did not get good grades.

The greatest reward for me being blessed with my special needs child happened to be his role as my spiritual guide. We started on a journey that led me to this day.

You will receive so many benefits day by day, month by month, and year by year while caring for your ASD child. If you interview parents of autistic children, they each tell a different story about the rewards and challenges they go through caring for their ASD children. But in the end, they all will say one common thing. Living with a child with autism is one of the best things that ever happened to them, and they would not change their life's experiences for any other experience.

CHAPTER 25

Tips for Caring for the Parents

Don't forget about self-care while caring for your autistic children. While caring for your children, you will need to incorporate self-care for yourself, or, else you will end up becoming exhausted. I always like to use the airplane analogy. You are all seated in the plane on the runway with your seat belt on. The air hostess makes the safety announcement;

> "Ladies and Gentlemen,
> Oxygen and air pressure are always being monitored. In the event of a decompression, an oxygen mask will automatically appear in front of you. To start the flow of oxygen, pull the mask towards you. Place it firmly over your nose and mouth, secure the elastic band behind your head, and breathe normally. Although the bag does not inflate, oxygen is flowing to the mask. If you are travelling with a child, or someone who requires assistance, secure your mask on first, and then assist the other person. Keep your mask on until a uniformed crew member advises you to remove it."

This statement makes perfect sense, how can you help the child or, the person who requires assistance before you put your own mask on? The same thing occurs when looking after your

ASD children; you need to look after yourself first, before you care for your child. This is not selfishness, it is called self-care or looking after number one in order to look after number two. You will need all the help and support for yourself, in order to look after your autistic child so you do not become exhausted.

When my teacher, Joshua Rosenthal, spoke about the concept of *primary foods*, I thought he was referring to food that we put in our mouth, but later on, I found out that primary foods are just as important as the food that we put in our mouth. We can eat all the fruits and vegetables that we like or, better still eat all the healthy foods we want; yet, if no balance exists in our lives, we will still be sick and stressed out. You see, all the other areas of your life have to be in synchrony, in order for you and your child to have that balance. We must address the other areas of our lives such as our relationships; our career even if it means a stay at home mom or dad; physical activity and our spirituality. By addressing these other areas of our lives and addressing the actual diet, you then create a balance for both you and your family; only then will you be able to find stability in your life.

I will now share my top twenty two *primary foods* tips with you, so that you will know how I created that balance in in my life.

1. Self-Care

The first tip to share with you focuses on taking care of yourself first and foremost. Care for self is not selfishness. If you think this is selfish, let me ask you one question, what do you do when you run yourself down and become exhausted? Who will take care of you? Who will take care of your child when you are not able to? Don't you think that life will go on? The universe always provides someone to take care of our children even when we are not able to do so. Therefore, it becomes imperative that you take time to care for yourself while in the process of caring for your ASD children.

One mother described feeling resentment for her child and when upset would take out her frustration on her child. Do you know why that is? The mother exhibited burnout. She lacked self-care. She said she needed to separate herself from her child for a week. She went on a vacation. While on the vacation, she felt guilty for feeling the way she did. Once she was back from the vacation, she felt better about herself and could start caring for her child once more without feeling any resentment.

2. Rest

Adequate rest is essential to restore your body's functions. You might ask me how you can obtain adequate rest when you are parenting a child with special needs. Below are some techniques to use in order to incorporate rest into your schedule.

When you need your rest, for those that can afford it, *hire a caregiver* to watch the children. For those who do not have the resources for hiring a caregiver, here are some recommendations:

- Ask a friend or family member to watch the kids for a few hours. If no one is available, team up with another parent of an autistic child and take turns watching each other's kids.
- Contact specific government agencies for help. As discussed earlier, the government does provide funding for some children along the spectrum to assist with respite care for parents, depending on the country you are living in. I would recommend that you speak to a member of your child's team to help you in accessing these services. Remember there is always an age limit for this type of funding (usually up to age eighteen); therefore; it is most beneficial to access these funding as early as possible.

- Take frequent naps: Have you ever felt very tired and you closed your eyes for a few minutes and before you know it, you drifted into a deep sleep? By the time you opened your eyes again, you felt renewed energy all ready to go again. This could be as little as five to ten minutes you spent napping and you are all ready to go again.

3. Physical Activities

Releasing stress is very crucial; you need some form of an outlet to release your stress, to retain your mental clarity and to maintain your focus.

You can enact some form of meditation, stretching, running, lifting weights, twenty minutes or more of brisk walking at least three to four times per week, going to the gym and performing other forms of workouts recommended by a fitness instructor, or, if you do not want to spend money on going to the gym, or, do not have a sitter for your child, you can dance. Put on your favorite piece of music and dance to it for about twenty to thirty minutes, just let yourself go and really dance. Don't worry if you look foolish. You will feel fantastic when you are finished and sometimes you will even laugh at yourself, but I guarantee you will feel much better when you stop. Who knows, your child might be in a mood to dance with you which would help them feel better about themselves as well.

It might be a little more difficult for a lower functioning ASD child to dance; however, just seeing you enjoy yourself might make them happy, as well.

4. Humor

Laugh frequently as it is said that laughter boosts the immune system and provides the best medicine. Watch funny movies, be funny, and keep company with funny people, sign up for laughter yoga classes and see the humor in every situation.

5. Date night

For the couples out there, sometimes we forget about our partners as we become so wrapped up in caring for our children. In the process, the partners feel neglected, become bored and eventually move on to find love elsewhere. This situation causes an even bigger problem as now the one parent left behind is struggling with the burden of taking care of the family by themselves. The parent left behind and child, have to deal with the extremely difficult separation process.

The children have to not only deal with separation from one parent, but also deal with their own issues. This state of affairs can be very frustrating for everyone involved. The child might start having more difficult, inappropriate behaviors and sometimes we fail to cue in on the fact that the child might be yearning for the other parent.

Think about a separation occurring in a family without a special needs child to deal with, just a regular child. You know how hard it is for the regular child to act, often developing emotional problems. It becomes even harder for a child who does not speak to express his sad feelings.

What I am trying to say is for you and your spouse to make time for each other. Participate in a date night at least once per month. Go to the movies or do the things you both enjoy doing. It can be anything from ballroom dancing to hanging out on a patio, whatever. Program it in your schedule whether it be weekly, bi-weekly or monthly; just do it to preserve your sanity and your relationship. By doing this, you will always have something to look forward to when the going gets tough. Maintaining balance in every aspect of your lives is paramount.

6. Taking vacations.

Take vacations as often as possible. It does not need to be an expensive vacation. It could be as simple as going somewhere for a week-end. You could go camping with the family or with just your counterpart. If you are going camping, watch out for the bugs and flies as some ASD children do not like insects. Week-end retreats represent a big one these days, wherein, you can just get away for the week-end and be pampered. Typically, we tell ourselves that we will take a vacation tomorrow, and tomorrow never comes. We say that we will get away when we retire, when the bills get paid, when the kids grow up, when little Johnny starts behaving, or, when this or that happens. You have to enjoy your life now as you only pass this way but once. Don't wait for retirement, or when the situation gets better, do it now and live a balanced life. Support each other. I remember reading a quote somewhere that says, "Remember it is not the finish that is important, but the journey that you are on."

For the parents, not in a relationship, you can still schedule time off and enjoy it with a friend. You need this special time so that you can just be yourselves and have that weekly or monthly event to look forward to. If finding someone to share the time with becomes difficult, several things come to mind that you can do like read your favorite book, go for nature walks, join a gym, go to a spa and get a massage, join a yoga class, go to the movie by yourself or invite a friend to go with you.

For the single fathers out there that are raising children along the spectrum by themselves, I want to say how much I respect and honor you. Not that I do not respect and honor the single mothers as well, but I think more single mothers exist looking after our children than single fathers, therefore, when we see a single father doing this job, we have to commend them because they share some of the same pain that we as mothers go through caring for our ASD kids.

Men need to schedule regular time off as well. Meet with your buddies, play a game of pool, golf or any other game you like. If for some reason you do not have a buddy, due to the fact that most of your time is spent caring for your children and working, you can always go to the gym and work out if you like doing that. These activities could be a great way to release your stress and give you renewed energy to come home and cope with caring for your children. There is so much you can do by yourself. Come to think about it, someone should form a social meeting group for single parents of ASD children. I think this group would be a hit as most of us can identify with each other and support each other.

7. Communicating with your spouse

Have regular conversations with your spouse. You will be able to express your feelings to each other, feel much better and even prevent resentment. I know that most men do not like to talk about their feelings; however, for all the fathers out there with children along the spectrum, I beseech you to start talking, talk to your wives, your partners, your parents; speak to anyone that you feel comfortable with expressing your internal feelings. This strategy will help you let things go instead of keeping them bottled up inside of you.

After talking about your feelings, you might find out that it is not so bad after all, and things could always be worse. Love and support each other. Remember that the beautiful man/woman you fell in love with sometime ago? It was just the two of you at the time. Now you both have a special needs child or, children in some cases. What are you going to do about it? This child has chosen you both to be her parents. Don't disappoint her by leaving one parent alone to bear the burden; stay and face up to the responsibility. Here is what I know, things can be very difficult at times, but I also know that good times occur as well. Hang in there, things will always get better.

Someone once related her story to me. She informed me that, when she reached four months in her pregnancy, her spouse told her that she better not be carrying a child with a disability, because if she did, he planned to leave. She told me that she could not understand why he would say that, she was really hurt. Eventually, she found out that his brother was autistic and her husband had a rough time growing up as a kid. Psychologically, this situation affected him very much and that explained the reason why he was fearful of having a child with a disability.

This upsetting situation happens when no education or counseling transpires at home about the subject of autism for the other family members who needed it. All the attention becomes focused on the autistic child and the other family members feel left out and neglected. I would recommend educating all family members about autism so that complete understanding occurs about what it is, how it affects other family members, and the limitations placed on the family members. In this way, they will understand the reason their autistic family member requires a lot of attention and why they need to divide up the chores of taking care of that individual.

8. Chores

Share the chores. Do not wait for one person to do all the work in a family with an autistic child. Take turns doing housework chores or do it together. Share the responsibility to prevent one person from becoming exhausted. Create a balance in your life. For the single parents, do take some time for yourself, you can always do the dishes tomorrow or clean the house later, but you must take some "ME" time for yourself to prevent yourself from becoming exhausted.

9. Your Diet

Detail diet discussion transpired earlier. Therefore; I will not spend a lot of time on this topic. What you put in your mouth remains vitally important. I will not dictate to you what you should eat, *as one man's picnic is another man's poison*, so to speak. Eat food that gives you energy as you will need energy to care for your children. Keep a food diary, record what you eat, detail how you feel a few hours after you ate, list the food that makes you feel sluggish and sick, and then eliminate the problem foods from your diet completely. As a dear friend of mine would say, "if you want to live, why put dead things in your body?"

Eat your veggies raw as much as possible as it helps you to get all the nutrients for life in their natural state. When you cook vegetables too much, you destroy the life and nutrients within them. We all know that we should eat more fruits and vegetables. Therefore, you don't need one more person telling you to eat your fruits and vegetables, do you?

As a matter of fact, you should be feeding the entire family healthy foods as you all will avoid health problems in the long run. Remember you are what you eat. As discussed earlier, forming a balance in you and your family's lives, require incorporating all the elements of the primary food circle as mentioned by Joshua Rosenthal. Only then will you find this balance.

If you are not getting enough nutrients from your food due to depletion of the nutrients, you should consider supplementing your diet with a high grade supplement that will provide you with the nutrients that you are lacking. Your family doctor should be able to help you by suggesting an appropriate multivitamin.

10. Sunlight

Expose yourself and your children to lots of sunlight when you can. In some parts of North America, it becomes very difficult to sunbath. Frequently, hardly any sunlight appears. During these times, supplementing with vitamin D3 provides this necessary nutrient. However, the best source still comes from direct sunlight. If you are living in any other part of the world wherein sunshine occurs all year round, you should be okay. Just apply sunscreen so you do not get sunburn.

11. Water

As discussed in an earlier chapter, keep an adequate supply of water on hand. I do not mean coffee, tea, juice, beer or pop. I mean plain water of high quality. Most of us suffer dehydration because we do not drink enough water. This explains why we get a lot of headaches and tire easily. The next time you feel a headache coming on; ingest a glass or two of water. If you feel hungry, before you open that cupboard to take out that snack, reach for a glass or two of water and drink it. You might find out that you don't feel hungry anymore or, the headache might go away. Our body is composed of 80% water and some of us do not drink an adequate amount of water, on a daily basis to maintain this level. Some people will tell you that they cannot drink a lot of water as it makes them go to the washroom too often. That could be the case, however, overtime that evens out and eventually your body becomes accustomed to drinking the water and the frequent trips to the washroom will decrease.

12. Just Breathe

Remember to practice deep breathing at least three times per day. Breathing occurs automatically, we do it every second, however; we might not be doing it correctly. When we do deep breathing, we get more air into our lungs and more oxygen to our brain. Here is one technique for deep breathing. Breathe in to a count of four, hold to a count of seven and breathe out to a count of eleven. Repeat this process three times and practice at least three times per day.

13. Support group

Develop or form a support group, especially for the mothers. Most women like to talk and while conversing, they release an abundance of their stress. They are not necessarily looking for advice; they just need someone to listen to them while they empty issues out of their head.

Soliciting a person to listen to you is so very crucial to your sanity. It could be a support group, a friend, a close family member or, you can hire a health counsellor to listen to you. The health counsellor can hold you accountable for the health goals that you set for yourself and the issues you wish to work out. For those who can afford it, I would definitely recommend that you hire a Certified Holistic Health Counsellor as they listen to you and do not judge you. You do not have to worry about them revealing confidential stories to others, because as professionals and a part of their ethical practice, they are not allowed to do so. Confidentiality becomes a big part of the agreement between you and them.

For those who work outside of the house, make sure that you enjoy your job, as it will be quite stressful if you do not. On top of working in a stressful environment all day, you then come home and having to deal with your child's issues especially those involving your child's school. For me, the school issues represented the worst of my child's problems that I had to deal with. I arrived home and read his communication book about the issues he had at school that day and that was very stressful for me.

Believe me, most of the time, the negative behaviors outweighed the positive behaviors. Therefore, it becomes imperative that you enjoy your job and, have substantial support individually, or, within a group.

14. Spirituality

Develop some form of spiritual practice that you can follow. I don't care if it is Christianity, Buddhism, Islamic, Taoist, Hinduism, or whatever. Just attach to a spiritual practice as you will need it. It helps you to see the bigger picture for your life and provides comfort when you are having one of those days and believe me you will experience challenging days.

Spend time practicing your spirituality on a daily basis. I find a quiet time first thing in the morning works for me before I communicate with anyone else. I spend time communicating with my God, my creator, asking for divine guidance for that day. Sometimes I will go for a walk in nature and I see God in the trees, the blue sky, the birds, and each creature. That is God's handy-work. Find what time of the day works best for you and do it.

When you have a strong faith, whatever struggles you are going through, you will possess the comfort to know that you are not alone and that this too shall past. What I have learned in life is that, the things we perceive as being bad in our lives are just road signs to get us to the next stage of our excursion on the journey of life. Our higher power tests us to see if we can handle the next stage of the journey ahead of us. Once we get through this stage, most of the time we can look back and say, now I know why that happened and why this happened. You realize the reason why you had to go through that test and you now become grateful for those difficulties that moved you forward.

When you are going through the testing stage, it is really difficult to see the blessings. All you want to say at that time is: "Why me Lord," but remember, things do get better and this too will pass.

Your child will observe you and learn that what he sees is a part of his life. It is said that children live what they learn.

I perceive that there is only one God, the God of this great big universe and we are each a part of this whole living experiences in this universe. We all play a role therein, I cannot do your job and you cannot do my job. We all have to play our part, in order to receive the complete experience. Maybe, just maybe, your role, or my role is to care for our autistic children and in the process grow to a higher level which will enable us to help others along the way.

15. Being grateful.

We should always be grateful for everything in life and we need to bring ourselves to a place in our lives, wherein we can express being grateful for everything, even the so called bad things.

We look at our situation and think that it is so bad. It is the worst thing that could ever happen to us. Why God, the Universe, or the Creator gave me a child with autism? Why me Lord, why me? Couldn't you have given me a normal child just like my friend Sue?

Instead of asking these questions and feeling sorry for ourselves, we should just observe other people's situation, and notice how blessed we are. I am not saying that you should compare yourself with others, but just think about it. Your child is alive and you can hug her whenever you want and tell her how much you love her. Think about a family who possesses a regular child. This child is on the honor roll at school, getting ready for university, or, already graduated from university as a doctor, lawyer, teacher etc., and, all of a sudden he passes away by some fluke accident. How do you think the parents feel? They can never get another chance to hug the child, or to tell the child how much they love him any longer. As one person said "life is like a game of poker, everyone gets a hand of cards and we have to play it to the best of our abilities." I cannot play your hand and you cannot play mine. We each have to play our own hand. So love your child, care for your child and be grateful for your hand with a special card, your autistic child.

Sometimes as humans, when things just spontaneously happen, we react to the situation in a negative way. However if we change our mindset as soon as possible, and bring ourselves back to a happy place, we start feeling good about ourselves once more, and start feeling grateful for what we have. When you think that way, it will totally change your mind set and take your mind away from problems and move it towards gratitude.

16. Give Thanks

One other thing you need to do each morning as you wake up is to thank your Creator, your God, the Universe whatever you call your spiritual higher power for waking you up. Just think about it, many other people did not wake up, but you received a second chance on life. Yesterday went on by and will not return to you. Tomorrow is not promised to you, so live in the moment. Be thankful for the opportunity to be given another day to be with your loved ones and to tell them how much you love them. Everything else is mind over matter.

17. Forgive.

The first person that you need to forgive is yourself. It clearly is not your fault that you have an autistic child. You represent a great parent and you did not do anything wrong. We, as parents, especially mothers, take things too personally and tend to want to fix everything. We try to fix it and when we can't fix it, we become frustrated, and, in turn highly stressed.

Some of us constantly carry that little piece of suffering in front of us and we block out, or forget about the good around us. Think about your life, what good things happened so far. Since you started this journey, think about the people you met and the places that you have gone. If you did not have a special needs child, would you have had those experiences? I tend to believe that this is your journey, our journey, and you and only you, can walk this path. Everyone else's journey is different and we all have to live our own experiences.

Once, you learn to forgive yourself, you have to start learning to forgive others that you felt did you wrong. The greatest accomplishment that you can achieve is letting go of your past, and the baggage that kept you trapped in your past. Start forgiving others and commence living from your heart. You will feel a sense of complete happiness and contentment. When you start forgiving, you will become a better person and people will see you as a new person. Your family and friends will all want to know what is going on and want to find out why you are so happy. This state of contentment is one of the biggest secrets in life. I can only tell you this because I tried it. These remedies helped me find true happiness on earth. What I learned revealed that the wrong done to me by others really was a way of helping me to grow and get to the next level. I am now learning to be thankful and grateful for everything that happened in my life. At first it may seem difficult, however, taking one step at a time, and then you can start living your authentic life.

18. Stop the blame and shame

Please stop beating up yourself. I am here now, at this present moment in time, to tell you to stop blaming yourself. You are a wonderful parent made by God in his Divinity. You are whole and perfectly made by him. No need to be ashamed of yourself. Hold your head up high when you walk, and remember to pat yourself on the back for being such an awesome parent.

19. Accountability partners.

Most people in the beginning have no problem changing their lifestyle. However, at one time or another, they end up falling back into the same old patterns and do not know why. It is similar to being on a diet, you get excited at first, and you lose five pounds, ten pounds or even more. However, overtime you start getting comfortable with yourself, start falling back into the old routines and habits and start putting on the weight again. One key ingredient is missing to keep you motivated and to keep you going. The key ingredient is an accountability partner.

If you do not have someone that will hold you accountable, and to help you achieve your lifestyle goals that you have set for yourself, I would recommend that you hire a certified Holistic Health Counsellor, or a Health Coach, as they are sometimes called. These professionals will help you to become a better person, in order to care for your autistic children and yourself. Hiring one would be a good investment. Since this concept is fairly new. You can conduct research on line or visit my website at www.healthcoachwinnie.com for more information.

20. Do something out of the ordinary

Most of us take life so very serious and becomes up tight that we forget how to live. Once in a while, I encourage you to do something out of the ordinary. As my teacher, Joshua Rosenthal recommends, "Be Bad". I do not mean for you to go out and break the law. Just live a little. For example, you have been watching what you eat for an entire week, maybe a month, three months, or six months and depriving yourselves of things. I encourage you to break the rule a little, by going out once in a while and order your favorite dessert. The rule of thumb recommends that you eat healthy eighty to ninety percent of the time and leave the other ten to twenty percent for days when you feel like having your special treat. It could be times when you are travelling, or just on the go and do not have the resources for eating healthy.

Try being yourself by telling someone what you really think of them. You know people that have been bullying you all your life and you feel intimidated by them. Find your voice in order to learn to speak to these offensive individuals. After you speak up, you will feel better and the other person might find out that he or she needs to reform their behavior. I am not saying that you should always be confrontational. At times, you need to stop being a people pleaser and find your inner voice in order to develop your confidence level so that you can advocate for you and your ASD children.

21. De-clutter

Are you a pack rat? Some people become collectors of things for years and never get rid of them. For instance, it could be a piece of clothing in your closet that you keep holding onto it, telling yourself that you are going to fit into it. But, it hung there for years taking up space and you still cannot fit into it. It could be your child's art work from kindergarten, or, your favorite magazines from many years ago, but whatever it is that you are holding on to that is no longer needed, you need to get rid of it. We collect things over the years, hoard them until our home becomes cluttered, but we still find it very hard to let go of our stuff.

I challenge you to do a cleansing. Get rid of the things that you no longer need. Maybe you can do a garage sale or donate them to the Salvation Army or Goodwill. Once your house is nice and clean you will feel so much lighter and your ASD children will feel better as well.

You should also unclutter your life. You know that person who only takes up space in your life like the piece of clothing in your closet. They stay there for no apparent reason. You do not hear from them when things are going well. Then you suddenly received a phone call that goes on and on forever, you become their dumping ground. Ask yourself these questions. What purpose do they serve in my life? By holding on to this person what am I achieving? By letting go what would it cost me, what would I lose? Once you find your answers, you can make your decision. Uncluttering your life, frees up more time for you to take care of your ASD children.

22. Cleanse your thought.

Now, it comes time to cleanse your thoughts. It is just like cleansing your house and your life. We acquire so many different thoughts in our mind and it is very hard to control them. Depending on what we are thinking, thoughts can become our feelings.

The goal requires you to assimilate positive feelings about yourself and your situation. When you are feeling sad or bad about yourself, or the situation, remember to stop yourself and ask, "What thoughts am I having now?" Once you have your answer, you will then be able to switch your thoughts in order to feel better. I am not saying that there won't be times when you have sad thoughts. For example, your child just had a meltdown at the shopping mall and you feel very bad. That situation is perfectly normal, but don't dwell on it for too long. It happened; it is done, move on now. Move on by using your energy to think about something positive, something that will benefit you and your child. I always tell myself that the situation could always be worse, and there are people who are in worse position than I am. People lay in the hospital and can't move; people who can't see the beautiful sunshine; etc.

I once attended a presentation wherein this gentleman presenter, had no hands, and he sat there giving the presentation, he brushes his hair with his feet and drinks from a cup with his foot holding the cup. When I saw him, I said to myself, I have nothing to worry about as I possess both my hands everything else is mind over matter.

My hope for you is that you will take a few of these tips mentioned in this chapter and apply them to your life in order for you to live a more fulfilling existence, while caring for your autistic children.

CHAPTER 26

What Happens To My Child When I Am No Longer Around?

Most of us worry about our children growing up and we express concern about other people taking advantage of them. Do the best you can as a parent to prepare your child for this world and to be independent as much as possible. Things will fall into place. We will not be here forever, therefore, we have to trust that they will be okay and that the universe will take care of them. Just do your part to provide for them as much as you can. Open a savings account for them, and if possible, do some form of investment for them, so that when you are gone there will be no misunderstanding about how they will be supported financially.

The biggest fear parents of autistic children have, is dying and leaving their children. They worry about who will take care of the children when they are no longer around. Will there be enough money to take care of them? They worry about people abusing their children and the list goes on. These circumstances can be quite challenging.

Some people set up trust funds to take care of their children. Do research on the different types of trusts and programs that are available to help these children. Find a trusted family member or a friend, one that is loyal and trustworthy to administer the funds for your children. Take out a life insurance policy and leave the trust as the beneficiary for your children. Make a living will. Once you have done all this, you will feel much better knowing that if you lost the ability to take care of your child, she would be well taken care of. This plan will relieve you of the additional burden of having to worry about that aspect of your life.

Conclusion

So here is the scoop, some of us will be able to see our children graduate from high schools, colleges or even universities and become productive members of society. You will be the proudest parents there is. You will know that you have done a fantastic job and know that you have fulfilled your job for this part of your journey. You will feel a big relief that your child has made it this far. You will be so happy that you stayed with your family in order to help your children to accomplish their goals together as a family. *Now what?* You are ready to help your children to accomplish another goal, the goal of living and functioning in the real world. They will need lots of support as they progress day by day working outside of the home, buying their first car, the day they move out into their own place, then getting married, having a family, having their first child. Some will continue to need your support right through life. The solution requires making them as independent as possible and eventually seeing them self-sufficient. This desired scenario will give you more time to live your life and to do the things that you always wanted to do, but could not do while they were still living at home.

For you the parents I articulate a big congratulation to you. You have done it, despite of all the challenges and now you know the secret to rearing a child on the spectrum. Don't keep this knowledge to yourself, share your story with someone who struggles like you did before, or, with someone just receiving a diagnosis of autism for their child and wondering WHAT NOW? You will be glad that you shared your story and that person will benefit significantly from your experiences. As part of our journey on this big planet earth, we are a part of the whole, the universe, and, we are here to help each other. This bigger vision is the reason to help others, because nobody can do our part like we do it. This remains one of the reasons why you were entrusted with such a huge job of rearing a child on the spectrum. God, the Universe knows how capable you are and that you can handle the job. Now, I encourage you to go ahead and share your story with others.

For some of us, we will be less fortunate, because our children will never be able to graduate from high schools, colleges or universities. I still say congratulations for coming this far. Instead, just think about the special moments that you had with your child, the laughter and the experiences that other moms do not get to have. Think about the lessons that you have learned the knowledge, the people you met and the friendships that you developed, and the love that you shared. Was it not worth it all? Had it not been for your ASD child, you would have never had this life experience and best of all you can hug your child and tell him how much you love him. Some parents will never have that opportunity.

You can share your stories with others who are ignorant about autism. You never know when you will become a blessing to someone else who is going through the journey that you have already gone through. Maybe, just maybe, that is your reason for coming to this planet earth, to have gone through the struggles of rearing your ASD child and gathering this knowledge to help someone who is going through the challenges and not knowing what to do. With your acquired knowledge, you will be able to help that individual and you will feel very happy that you have helped a family in need. My prayer is that; after reading this book, you will never have to say these words: "Autism diagnosis, what now?"

Namaste.

About the Author

As a Certified Holistic Health Counsellor and AADP certified, **Winnifred Matilda Walcott** is the founder and CEO of Health Coach Winnie Health Counselling. She remains deeply passionate about helping and showing other parents and caregivers, who are living and working with individuals along the Autism Spectrum, how they can live happier lives by finding a balance, despite the challenges they encounter daily with their ASD children.

One client describes her as the most positive and up-beat person she has ever met, who gets the job done and still catches time to relax. When she is not busy speaking and writing, you can find her at her country home, working on setting up her holistic health retreat for busy moms and dads of ASD children.

When Winnifred Matilda Walcott first received her son's diagnosis of ASD/PDD, her first words were "What now?" Even though she was hoping and praying that the doctors would finally come up with the right diagnosis for her child, when she received the diagnosis, she felt confused and frustrated. She went into self-denial. She started blaming herself for letting her child develop autism. She blamed the God/the universe, and asked "How could you let my child develop autism?" She would not speak openly to anyone about her child for fear that others would think that she was an incompetent mom.

One day she suddenly realized that, she was heading for a nervous breakdown, caring and worrying about her teenaged old autistic son and the rest is the history in this book.

Index

ABA, 92
Accountability, 138
ADHD, 13, 35-36, 51
Advocating, 10, 42-43, 117, 121, 138
Antipsychotic Drugs, 92
ASD, 120, 122, 124-126, 128-129, 139-140, 145, 147
Behaviors, 49, 55, 70, 80, 83, 85-89, 92-94, 96, 108-109
Billy, 19-20, 23 53
Birthdays, 71
Boundaries, 67
Breathe, 14, 16, 57, 123, 139
Bullying, 52, 69, 70, 98, 139
Caregiver, 21, 24, 35, 62, 76, 94, 106, 147
Chores, 130
Cleanse, 140
Clutter, 30, 139
Competitiveness, 31
Confidentiality, 133
Cytokines, 52
Date night, 127
Dentist, 37-38, 73-74
Diet, 32-33, 38, 52, 55- 57, 60, 88-89, 91, 113, 124, 131, 136, 138.
Discipline, 24, 45, 47, 84, 118
Echolalia, 30

Education, 4, 14, 20, 24-25, 34-35, 37, 39-42, 67, 80, 91, 93, 96, 100, 101, 122, 130
Eye Contact, 22, 63
Family, 10, 11, 13
Finding your path, 122
Glutathione, 89-91
GDD, 13
Gratitude, 10-11, 17, 122, 136
Health Coach, 37, 39, 138, 147
Hidden allergen, 52
Home School, 98
Housing, 108
Humor, 126-127
Hyperbaric Changer 91, 93
Homework, 99-100
IEP, 100, 101
Impairment, 20, 36, 86, 110
Impulsivity, 24, 25, 59
Love, 7, 9, 10, 42, 43
Meetings, 97, 101-102, 117, 122
Meltdowns, 44-45, 47
Multiple Diagnosis, 35
Nutraceutical 91
Obsession, 28
Nutraceutical, 91
Pacing, 31, 49
PDD, 10, 13, 40, 51, 147
Pediatrician, 33, 37, 40, 43, 57
Perlmutter, Dr. David, 52

Potty Training, 76
Primary Foods 39, 124
Psychologist, 37, 39-41, p4
Repetitive Behaviors, 33
Rosenthal, Joshua, 10, 56, 124, 131, 139
Self-care, 112
Self-injury, 83
Sibling, 74, 77, 116, 118
Snoezelen room, 48
Social kills, 21, 79 93, 94, 98

Spirituality, 113, 124, 134
Speech therapy, 91, 93
Sugar, 51-52, 55-56, 58, 88
Sunlight, 132
Support group, 41, 68, 133
Team, 31, 36-38, 40, 42-43, 93, 103-104, 125
Transitions, 31, 47, 85
Visual Based therapy, 95
Water, 98 50, 57-58, 132
Williams, Donna, 112

www.ingramcontent.com/pod-product-compliance
Lightning Source LLC
LaVergne TN
LVHW051606070426
835507LV00021B/2788